tai chi
odyssey

History
and
Practice
Methods

太
極
拳

An Anthology of Articles from the Journal of Asian Martial Arts

Compiled by Michael A. DeMarco, M.A.

Articles in this anthology were originally published in the *Journal of Asian Martial Arts*, and from *Asian Marital Arts: Constructive Thoughts & Practical Applications* (2013) Listed according to the table of contents for this anthology:

Cover illustration
Michael DeMarco practicing Xiong-style Taiji straight sword.
He teaches in Santa Fe, NM, and at workshops in the USA and abroad.
www.wingedliontaichi.com
Photograph ©2016 by Jose Leon Castillo, III. www.castilloimages.com

ISBN-13: 978-1893765474
ISBN-10: 1893765474

contents

preface

This anthology offers not only a handy historical overview of taijiquan history, but most chapters focus on actual practice. Guidance is provided through Carol Derrickson's discussions on taijiquan classic writings as well as from other highly experienced instructors in their own chapters.

Dr. Linda Lehrhaupt's chapter inspires one to practice by explaining how mental changes occur in a student during initial weeks of classes. Although most taiji classes are offered by individuals in their own schools, a number of classes are also offered in academic settings. Andrew Peck gives a fine example of how taiji is taught in a university setting.

Other authors present subtle aspects of practice—be it eye movement, circles that exist even in movements that appear to be liner, benefits derived from solo and group practice, or the too often elusive element of relaxation. All these chapters will prove valuable to anyone wishing to improve their quality of practice and thus to reap more health benefits taiji has to offer. The same embodied principles can be utilized in martial applications, if one chooses.

Peter Lim wrote two chapters. In one he details general taiji principles that are put into the practice, while in the other chapter he looks specifically at how the principles can be applied in combat. His chapters provide a solid foundation for better understanding *tuishou*, the two-person push-hands practice that Herman Kaus and Hal Mosher (with the help of Allen Pittman) discuss. Greg Wolfson (with the help of Scott Rodell) writes about push-hands and *sanshou*—a high-level two-person practice of combative training. Russ Mason's short but pertinent chapter samples two favorite techniques: wardoff and diagonal flying.

The chapters by Donald Mainfort and Joel Stein are relatively unique in that they look at the variety of taiji forms—contrasting the original Chen Style with the Yang Style, and the large and medium frames—helping us better understand how and why routines differ, and which may be better suited for particular individuals. As a result, we can also see why movements from different styles can blend into anyone's practice.

Comprised of articles previously published in the *Journal of Asian Martial Arts*—we are highly optimistic that you will find something on each page of this anthology to be of great use in your understanding and practice.

Michael A. DeMarco, Publisher
Santa Fe, New Mexico, November 2017

The Origin and Evolution of Taijiquan
by Michael A. DeMarco, M.A.

Taijiquan enthusiasts arrive in Taipei's 2/28 Peace Park before sunrise, benefiting from their practice in an atmosphere of fresh air and tranquility. Later in the morning, disco-style exercisers arrive to gyrate in beat with blaring disco music. Somehow, all seems to blend harmoniously in the typical fashion of Chinese yin-yang sociology. Small surprise that there is also quite a stylistic variety in taijiquan as well. Photo by M. DeMarco

> I am not one who was born
> in the possession of knowledge;
> I am one who is fond of antiquity,
> and earnest in seeking it there.
> *Confucian Analects*, 7: 19

History, according to the Chinese tradition, is not to be understood as a passage of time toward a perfect human state. On the contrary, it is seen as a regression away from a splendid "Golden Age" when their ancestors lived in a utopian state more than four thousand years ago. All things wise and good were believed to have existed during this period. It represented a period which held secrets for proper living, supreme health and happiness. Even for the martial arts, what is deemed most worthy is held to be the creation of sagacious warriors of antiquity.

The Chinese fanatical respect for antiquity presents some formidable barriers for any student of their culture. It was a common practice for many Chinese writers to falsely assign their works to an earlier time in order to gain greater respect and fame for their works. Sometimes, besides placing their works in an earlier period, writers would credit a work as being "brushed" (they did not use pens yet!) by an earlier figure of prestige. Oftentimes the work would be anonymous, not dated, not punctuated, and filled with incomprehensible symbolic jargon. This certainly occurred in martial art literature as well. Trying to trace the origin of a boxing system can cause a researcher to perform a wonderful assortment of kicks and punches simply out of academic frustration!

Taijiquan, as part of the cultural history of China, is encrusted in a confusing maze of facts and fiction. This is a reality which needs constant attention in studying the history of any martial art. The following theories on the origin of taijiquan show how myth and legend are blended within the Chinese cultural heritage. Fortunately, with a critical eye for reliable data, we can present a sound overview regarding the evolution of taijiquan.

Theories of Early Dynastic Origin

One theory states that taijiquan originated during the end of the Liang Dynasty (502-557 CE) and the beginning of the Chen Dynasty (557-589 CE). These dynasties had their capital at Nanjing in present-day Jiangsu Province on the Yangtze River.

Another theory holds that the creation of taijiquan came slightly later, during the Tang Dynasty (618-907 CE). The Tang capital is situated in present-day Shaanxi Province. Then called Changan, the great city is now referred to as Xi'an. It is the place where the famed life-sized terra cotta warriors, which marked the grave site of China's First Emperor of Qin, were recently unearthed.

In placing the origin of taijiquan at such early periods, the two theories stated above lack solid verification. These seem to be attempts to place the time of origin to an early era simply for added prestige. If these theories were accepted, a period in the history of taijiquan representing hundreds of years would be left vacant.

There is no doubt that many boxing schools existed during these early dynastic times, but their connection to the creation of taijiquan remains a remote root of the evolutionary tree of boxing. Taijiquan clearly comes into being as a later branch in the development of martial arts.

Zhang Sanfeng.
Ink rubbing of the legendary
founder of taijiquan.

Zhang Sanfeng as Possible Inventor

Many of today's taijiquan teachers will state that their art is derived from the system of Zhang Sanfeng. According to popular belief, he was a famous Daoist living on Mount Wudang in Hebei Province, a master of internal alchemy, and a boxer of the highest grade. Because of his fame, he was invited to the Imperial court by three different Emperors. Although he never did appear after numerous attempts to find him, he was canonized in 1459 by the Emperor Yingzong. There is a shrine in Beijing dedicated to "the Immortal Sanfeng" in the well-known White Cloud Monastery of the Quanzhen Daoist sect.

Most writings describe Zhang Sanfeng, alias Junbao, as an extraordinarily tall bearded figure, with large eyes. His feats of magic included riding through the air on a crane, and he could be at different places at the same time. It is even believed that after he died in the 1390's, he miraculously came back to life once again.

All of these accounts regarding Zhang Sanfeng serve to add an aura of semi-religious awe for the god-like creator of taijiquan. There are Zhang Sanfeng spirit-medium cults in China, particularly in the province of Sichuan. Nonetheless, in official bibliographies there is no mention of him even practicing taijiquan. Perhaps the most scholarly article in the English language on this subject was written by respected sinologist Anna Seidel, who states:

3

His biographies and legends lack even the faintest allusion to his being a boxing master... We know next to nothing about [Zhang] Sanfeng's historical existence and his thought. (484)

Once faced with the facts, the story of Zhang Sanfeng turns into a symbolic legend which represents the unknown influences that have contributed to the birth of taijiquan. As the patron of this style, the Daoist Zhang Sanfeng parallels the role Bodhidharma plays as the Buddhist patron of the Shaolin boxing school. The Daoist sanctuary on Mount Wudang was dedicated to the God of War named Chen Wu. This god was of supreme importance in war-ridden China during the Ming Dynasty (1368-1644). Despite the contradicting facts, many continue to believe that it was this god who revealed the art of taijiquan to Zhang Sanfeng in a dream.

The technique of attributing the origin of taijiquan to Zhang Sanfeng is just one illustration of the Chinese use of antedating. In so doing, taijiquan is given the respect of antiquity and the sacredness of a para-normal manifestation. Zhang represents an ideal boxing master with super-normal abilities. Believed to have lived for at least two centuries, he is often credited with creating the most efficient boxing system known.

Zhang Sanfeng's story fits in well with the popular beliefs prevalent during the Ming Dynasty. The thought of the time was influenced by Daoism, particularly the beliefs in immortals and esoteric techniques for self-cultivation. Through all the uncertainty, we eventually arrive at a point in time when taijiquan is taught and practiced. It is beyond all doubt that taijiquan was practiced in a Henan village more than 200 years ago. In this small commune, known as Chenjiagou, it is still practiced today. The known masters living there give no mention of Zhang Sanfeng as part of the taijiquan tradition, but present their own theory of origin.

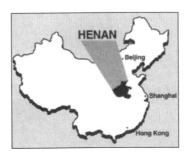

Peoples Republic of China showing the central location of Henan Province.

4

Above: Location of Xin Prefecture and adjoining provinces around Henan.

Below: Details of western Xin Prefecture. For the area outlined in the slanted square below, compare with following Space Shuttle photo.

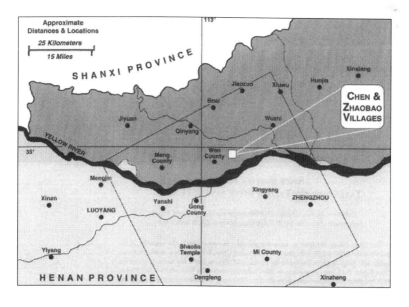

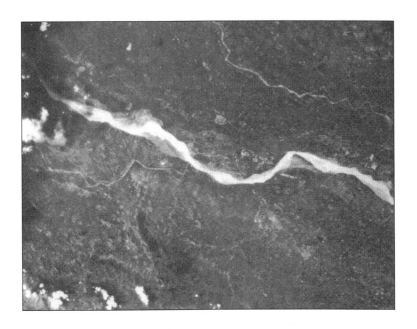

Space shuttle photo taken over the Yellow River, August 11, 1989.
Compare with map on page 12. Photograph available from the U.S. Department of the Interior, U.S. Geological Survey EROS Data Center. The Chen village obtained its name for the sake of convenience: the majority of the approximately 1,800 people living there are surnamed Chen. It is actually a small commune, roughly 400 miles south of Beijing in the province of Henan. Just a few miles north of the Yellow River, the Chen commune is in Xin Prefecture under the Wen administrative unit. This is less than one hundred miles from the city of Luoyang, which was previously a dynastic capital and a great cultural center.

Origination at Chen Village

For those who have not been swayed by the emotional attraction of placing the origination of taijiquan in either the early dynastic periods or at the time of Zhang Sanfeng, the theory that it originated in the Chen villages seems a more likely alternative. Here we find an exact location, verified dates, known boxing masters, and a clearly applicable historic setting for its origin.

The Chen village plays a unique role along with Henan province in China's historical development. In the most remote times, this area spawned one of China's earliest Stone Age cultures. By the 11th century, Luoyang was one of two metropolitan areas with a population of over one million people. Because of its riches, the area was often subject to barbaric invasions as well as internal rebellion.

6

In contrast to the external threats, internal problems were usually caused by peasant dissatisfaction resulting from natural and political disasters. The rapid increase in population during the later dynasties placed greater burdens on the Henan people. They had to face floods and food shortages, as well as exploitation by those holding political power. By 1600, about half of the provincial lands had been given to friends and relatives of the Imperial house as gifts or rewards. This abusive practice uprooted many peasants from their land.

The social structure of the Chen clan illustrates many features prominent among other small communes attempting to solve similar problems. One result of the insecure political situation during the Ming/Qing dynasties is that small groups of related people would bind themselves together into their own social unit. They organized themselves around a village leader and set up a communal system which would provide for their every need. Their major concern was focused on having sufficient amounts of food and water. But in a time of incessant warfare, rebellion and banditry, knowledge of the martial arts became a necessity for the protection of one's farm, home and family.

It is not surprising that the Shaolin Monastery, like the Chen village, is located in Henan Province. The monastery is about fifty miles southeast of the former capital of Luoyang. Other clans became noted for their own styles of boxing, but the Shaolin Temple and the Chen clan became the most famous for their superior systems. The monastery was also a social unit which had need of protecting its agricultural lands and religious art treasures. Likewise, the Chen village formed its own small protective group within society. In doing so, it placed emphasis on developing a martial art useful for the defense of its inhabitants against any outsiders, regardless of their boxing system.

Numerous theories have been stated which attempt to tie the Chen village in with the creation of taijiquan. By trying to find the earliest point in time when taijiquan was formed, we are presented with the scantiest of facts. One figure we find with substantial documentation is Wang Zongyue.

Wang Zongyue was a native of Shanxi, the province just north of Henan. It is said that he introduced a new form of boxing to the people of Chenjiagou when he stopped for a while in the village during his travels. This was said to have occurred during Emperor Qianlong's reign (1736-1795). A school teacher by profession, Wang was a learned man, credited with linking the original thirteen postures into a continuous sequence. In so doing, he applied the Daoist philosophy and concepts of yin/yang to the new style. One book, the *Taijiquan Lun*, is reputedly his work. In it is found the first mention of taijiquan as the formal name given to this system.

Wang Zong from Shaanxi Province is often confused with Wang Zongyue from Shanxi. The former is believed to be a disciple of the legendary Zhang Sanfeng. Because of the similarity of names and as an attempt to push the taijiquan lineage back further in time, Wang Zongyue is sometimes said to have learned his art from Zhang Sanfeng. Wang, living during a much later period, could not have been a student of Zhang.

Regardless of the confusion surrounding Wang Zongyue, there is little doubt about his influence at Chenjiagou. Since the village was already famed for its boxing, there is the greatest probability that a synthesis of styles took place. This seems to be the case because Wang only affected a Chen style that had been previously developed.

Although Wang Zongyue is credited with the first mention of the name taijiquan, we are primarily concerned with the evolution of the boxing form itself. Formerly it was known as *Zhangquan*, or Long Fist. By tracing the style prevalent at Chenjiagou during the time when Wang Zongyue was visiting, we find that a particular style had already been in existence there for a number of years.

Chen Wangting, alias Zouting, is credited as the true founder of the Chen style taijiquan. It is estimated that he lived from 1597 to 1664 and was a garrison commander in the Wen county where the Chen village is located. A military man, Chen absorbed many noted styles during his travels. Later he created his own style.

According to significant historical data and fables, Chen Wangting has received recognition as the true inventor of taijiquan and the "push-hands" exercises. Adopting and modifying movements from many martial art styles, plus tempering these movements with his own wisdom, he created the Chen system. Chen's new syncretic forms were to be performed in a fashion compatible with the then prevalent theories of Daoism.

Chen Wangting was the ninth generation heir of the Chen family, which was to carry on his unique boxing style to the present day. About 95% of the villagers living there today practice at least one of the forms originally taught by Chen himself. But this Chen style, originally so secretive, has moved outward from its place of origin with the passing of years. Until roughly one hundred years ago, taijiquan was largely practiced only in Henan province. Since then, it has swept to the four quarters of China and then into overseas areas where Chinese have immigrated.

Although it is the more modern Yang Style that is popular throughout the world, the Chen Style is also making its move into other areas outside of

China proper. But this is on a much less noticeable scale, for the Chen Style of taijiquan was always a rare style, even in China. It was a style reserved only for a select few. For this reason, the Chen Style is a relatively uncommon martial art system whose exceptional traits are know more from hearsay than from actual experience.

Masters and Evolution

In tracing the lineage of taijiquan, we can take an analytical approach by starting with the present-day masters and work our way back through time. By doing this, we amass an overpowering list of teachers and students. Many of the teachers are mediocre, to mention nothing of the students. There are only a few teachers of major significance. These are the masters who have truly developed the art of taijiquan.

The following chronology illustrates just how the various styles emerged from the original in light of the historic setting. It also presents the preservation of the Chen style through the direct lineage.

There is a confusing array of taijiquan styles including the Yang, Chen, Woo, Hao, Sun and Wu. Plus there are additional distinguishing adjectives such as the new, old, big frame, simplified, small frame, and an assortment of newly imagined styles. Like a substitute for a Chinese "water torture," we are supposed to bear the burden of figuring out how all these styles are related. As an additional hindrance, many of the names are found presented only in the Chinese rendering.

Chen Wangting

In a temple at Chenjiagou there is a painting of Chen Wangting, honoring him as the founder of the system. It is logical that the founder would not be a "Zhang" as Zhang Sanfeng, or a "Wang" as Wang Zongyue. As a rule, Chen Wangting's system was to be handed down only to descendants of the Chen family. While his original forms have largely been preserved through direct lineage, variations have occurred with time, some becoming separate styles in their own right.

The Chen style has been carried on through private instruction, passing from teacher to student over the past two centuries. This style was rarely presented in public. Literature regarding the subject has likewise been scanty. It was a highly secretive art form, requiring oral instructions from a master.

Today, the seclusive tradition which surrounds the Chen Style has apparently changed. People may think that because there is some literature and demonstrations of Chen Taijiquan that it is now openly presented to the public. Upon closer examination, what was written is found to present only a limited view of the system as a whole. Visual presentations usually consist of the basic form which, impressive in itself, is only an introduction to other sets.

Chen Wangting, previous to developing his own style, was influenced by a general Qi Jiguang, who reputedly designed a routine consisting of 32 movements which he synthesized from sixteen boxing styles. Chen, in turn, combined 29 of these movements with others and used them to form a total of seven different routines. Five of these were rudimentary, from which one remains as a standard routine for junior students.

Movements in the first routine are practiced with the feet leading the hands. The second routine is characterized with hand movements leading. Another noted feature is that there is a greater percentage of harder movements in the second routine. A later development, a third routine, attempts to perfectly blend the hard and soft movements in harmonious physical orchestration.

The style that Chen Wangting created was a physical embodiment of Daoist philosophy, particularly the concept of yin/yang. His system is a harmonious blending of hard/soft, fast/slow, passive and active. Within the yin there is potential yang, and vice versa. One of the Chen routines is called *Paochui*, or the "Cannon Fist." This term describes the intrinsic power present in Chen Wangting's system. The cannonball sitting in a stationary barrel becomes an active, hard-hitting projectile due to the explosive power inherent in its design. Chen Wangting developed such a system for his martial art, always potent with power.

Compared to all other styles of taijiquan, the Chen Style is also the most strenuous to practice. It includes very difficult leg work, utilizing squats, leaps and various kicks. Often there are changes in tempo. Movements include a circling and twisting of the waist known for producing "cork-screw strength" and "twisting energy." A hand strike, for example, actually starts from the heels allowing energy to move through the legs, waist, torso, shoulders, arms, and then into the hands. The end result is a blow stemming from the whole body, not just muscular power from one arm.

There are many features common to all taijiquan styles. However, a distinguishing feature of the Chen Style is its unique employment of physical laws to ensure maximum power for boxing. This is illustrated, for example, in the perfect alignment of the index finger to the elbow. The hand and arm form a straight line. Whether the hand formation is open or closed, the wrist should not be bent in any way. This plum line straightness is paramount in the Chen Style's use of the hands and can also be seen in the upright posture of the spine. It provides maximum power and safety from possible injury which could otherwise result during combat.

Regarding footwork, there is also a difference from other styles. In the posture called "Rooster Stands on One Leg," for example, the foot of the raised leg points directly forward with the sole parallel to the ground. This movement differs from the Yang Style where the toe points downwards. This simple variance is utilized for additional power as when used for a knee strike to an opponents mid-section.

The examples above show some of the unique features embodied in Chen Taijiquan. These movements include a large spectrum of fighting techniques: numerous open and closed hand strikes, qinna holds, jumping kicks, kicking from low postures, throws, and a wide assortment of blocks. During each set, special attention is given to one's technique, including the duration of the routine, strength developed, changes in rhythm and use of breathing.

Chen Wangting's system of taijiquan has been preserved through direct lineage from his time to the present day. In order to distinguish his original style from later branches of taijiquan, it is simply referred to as *Laojia*, or the "Old Family" system. A few other major schools which branched out from this direct lineage will be discussed later.

The Chen Lineage

The next major figure of the *Laojia* is Chen Changxing (1771-1853). He was the 14th generation grandmaster who lived in Chenjiagou and was directly descended from the founder. Because of his upright posture and revered character, he was referred to as "Mr. Name Board" (comparing him to a board which listed ancestors names, an object of great respect). Chen Changxing is also remembered as the teacher of Yang Luchan, who later founded the now popular style associated with his family name. Although this new-found branch began at this time, the mainstream of Laojia continued in its own familial succession.

We can see how selective Laojia masters are by observing the style's lineage. Chen Changxing was the direct descendant of the founder. He, in turn, as the 14th generation grandmaster, passed his knowledge on to his son, Chen Gengyun. This 15th generation grandmaster served as a military guard for the gentry class in Shandong Province. He became well-known for providing security for the Chinese upperclass, while his name became a symbol of law and order. The law was enforced through his superior martial prowess, or simply through the fear of it.

The son of Chen Gengyun, who became the 16th generation Grandmaster, was Chen Yenxi. Following in his father's footsteps was no easy task. Chen Gengyun was held in such prominence that a monument was dedicated to him along a Shandong road that was used to transport the rich cargo he protected for the gentry. The governor of the province, upon seeing this monument, decided to seek out Chen Gengyun to ask him to teach his children the Old Chen Style. Since Chen Gengyun had already died a few years previous, Chen Yenxi was commissioned for the task.

One significant aspect of Chen Yenxi giving instruction to the children of Shandong's governor is that the governor was to become a famous figure in China's history. His name was Yuan Shikai, a political-military man having great influence in the events which were to shape China's future.

Yuan was a pivot in the power struggles in the Beijing capital. He was the leading military figure in north China who at one time declared himself Emperor and also became the President of the new republic. Yuan met Chen during the final days of the Qing Dynasty. In this period of tragic disunity, China was plagued by revolutions, rebellions, and foreign intervention. Shortly after the Boxer Rebellion of 1900, warlords carved up the land in proportion to their own military strength and political cunning.

The significance of Yuan Shikai's asking Chen Yenxi to teach his family reinforces the belief that the Laojia Chen Style had gained a reputation as the most fearsome of all fighting systems. The Chen family name was already legend in places far distant from Henan Province.

There is another interesting note regarding a student of Chen Yenxi named Du Yuze (1896-1990). Du was the son of Du Yueh, the leading official in charge of the Henan country where the Chen village is located. Du, originally from Boai city located north of Chenjiagou, later moved to Taiwan. From among his list of students, he selected a few to become his adopted "sons" to carry on his inherited taijiquan tradition. More details regarding Du's life can be found in a booklet written by his "number one adopted son," Wang Jiaxiang, dedicated to Master Du for his 82rd birthday.

Next in the family lineage was Chen Fake (1887-1957), the son of Chen Yenxi. Chen Fake, the 17th generation grandmaster, went to Beijing in 1920 on personal business. There he became the first master of the Chen system to teach publicly. It was noticed, however, that he had changed the content and way of practicing the routines. It is most probable that his instruction to university classes differed from what he presented in private.

In Beijing, Chen Fake was often confronted with challenges from noted masters of various styles. Although he himself was a gentleman of great self-control, in instances of persistent antagonism, the fierceness of his system would prove overwhelming once unleashed. Defeated masters, such as Xu Yusheng, would acknowledge Chen Fake's superiority and sometimes humble themselves enough to become his students. Chen could defend himself with ease, but refrained from hurting his opponents.

Chen Fake's public teachings have continued in their changed form under such teachers as Tian Xiuchen and Kan Guixiang in Beijing. The Laojia system has been retained hereditarily. Chen Zhaoquai inherited the system, becoming the 18th generation grandmaster. He was Chen Fake's second son who carried on the tradition until his death in May, 1981.

The current grandmaster and, therefore, the 19th in order is Chen Xiaowang. As the grandson of Chen Fake, he is the living embodiment of the Laojia system. He recently developed a simplified Chen exercise comprised of 38 forms which is gaining popularity in the People's Republic of China. The present Chen Style influence has also reached the United States. A student under Chen Zhaoquai, Gene (Ching Hong) Chen, presently teaches in San Francisco. Gene Chen is the Chairman of the Chen Taijiquan Association of America.

From the taijiquan mainstream, representing the Chen lineage beginning with Chen Wangting, a clear picture can be drawn which illustrates where other styles emerged. In addition to the Laojia Chen system, the *Xinjia*, or "New Family" system is among the earliest variants.

The Xinjia, Wu, Hao, and Sun Styles

Chen Yuben and Chen Yuheng were twins who inherited taiji from the founder Chen Wangting. Chen Yuben is credited with changing the Laojia forms to make a "New Family" system, or *Xinjia*, composed of 83 forms. Yuben passed this new style on to his son, Chen Zhungshen (1809-1871). A long list of students followed this teaching, most bearing the Chen family name. This style, although differing from the Laojia, made the Chen style more available to the public. Chen Ziming and Chen Chunyuan were the leading figures of the Xinjia until the middle of this century.

Another student of Chen Yuben was Chen Qingping (1795-1868), who created a style characterized by small movements largely derived from Xinjia. It is referred to as *Xiao* (Small) Jia, or *Zaobaojia*, Zaobao being the village where Chen Qingping lived. Because a great portion of his students did not bear the Chen surname, we find later styles of taijiquan classified under other surnames.

Immediately after Chen Qingping comes a series of newly formed schools. The founders of these schools modified the taijiquan as taught by their teachers, re-naming their new methods according to their own surnames. The list of innovators includes Wu Yuxiang, Hao Weizheng and Sun Lutang.

Wu Yuxiang (1812-1880) was from a village in the southern part of Hebei Province, Hantan Prefecture. The founder of the Yang Style, Yang Luchan, was also from this village. A wealthy store owner, Wu Yuxiang had employed Yang as an assistant. He also hired Chen Changxing to teach his sons the Chen style. Wu was fortunate to have studied the Laojia style from Chen Changxing and the Xinjia by Chen Qingping before his own Wu style took shape.

The brother of Wu Yuxiang was Wu Chengching, a magistrate in central Henan Province, who reportedly found a rare treatise on taijiquan in a salt store and purchased it for his brother. The author was believed to be Wang Zongyue, the martial art practitioner said to have visited Chenjiagou in the mid-18th century. Wu Yuxiang himself wrote at least five articles regarding the practice of taijiquan.

Some of the Chen style can be seen within the Wu system, incorporating energetic movements such as a forward jump kick executed while slapping ones toes. Wu taught Li Yiyu (1883-1932), who was his sister's son. Another student of his was Hao Weizheng (1849-1920). Actually derived from the Wu school, the Hao style takes its name from Hao Weizheng who popularized this particular branch of taijiquan. Hao Yuehju, Hao Weizheng's son, carried on this tradition but deleted some of the more strenuous movements derived from the Chen style.

Born in Baoding, Hebei Province, Sun Lutang (1861-1932) was a student of Hao Weizheng. Sun's style required much flexibility and was fairly fast paced, reminiscent of the Chen system. For some time Sun lived in Beijing. Approaching 70 years of age, he was made Chairman of the Jiangsu Province Boxing Association. The Sun Style is also known as the *Huo Bu Jia*, or the "Lively Pace" Style.

Thus, the major schools of taijiquan classified under the surnames Wu, Hao and Sun were all derived from the Xinjia Chen system as founded by Chen

Yuben. In addition to this branch, two other styles have been recognized as major schools: the Yang and a Wu style which is not affiliated with the school of Wu Yuxiang. Within the overall evolutionary development of taijiquan, these schools emerge under special conditions which fostered their unique characteristics and popularity among the masses.

The Yang School Lineage and Branches

Why is the Yang Style the most popular of taijiquan styles? Because of its superior fighting techniques? Greater health benefits?... Many such questions are answered with the understanding of who the style's founder actually was, how he gained his knowledge, and how he passed on this knowledge.

Yang Luchan (1799-1872), also known as Yang Fukui, was a native of Hebei Province, Hantan Prefecture, Yunglienxien administrative unit. Here, the founder of the Wu style, herbalist Wu Yuxiang, also lived. As mentioned previously, Yang worked for Wu, and it was through this connection that Yang had the opportunity to learn the Chen style. Yang's relative, Li Pokui, also was employed here.

Yang began to learn taijiquan by practicing the movements he secretly observed while Chen Changxing taught Wu's sons. The discovery of Yang's ability to learn taijiquan so well by simply watching the lessons encouraged Chen to accept him as a student. Yang was a natural. Under the tutelage of Master Chen, Yang became a master in his own right. It is believed that Yang spent a total of 18 years at Chenjiagou. In later years, Yang went to the capital city of Beijing where he soon earned the nickname "Unbeatable Yang." This was due to Yang's defeating numerous famed boxers. Some stories say that after 18 masters had challenged him, Yang remained "untouchable."

When he went to Beijing, Yang gave public instruction in the art of taijiquan. But, it must be remembered the style he taught was not the same as those systems he himself learned. Beijing was the capital of China, which during the Qing Dynasty was ruled by the Manchus, not the Chinese themselves! The Manchurian Royalty, upon hearing of the famed boxer, asked for instruction. Yang taught Manchus and others, although he did not include the fast, powerful movements associated with his studies of the Old Chen system. He concentrated only on the yin movements, which were slow and soft. In so doing, he created a new style which helped taijiquan become known for its therapeutic benefits.

Although what Yang taught publicly was largely health oriented, his private teachings must have included his philosophy and techniques for self-defense. After all, he did teach the Emperor's guards! It would be hard to imagine such warriors wasting their time on a martial art without effective fighting techniques.

Proof that Yang Luchan had passed on a formidable fighting art is exemplified in the lives of his sons, Yang Jianhou (c.1839-1917) and Yang Banhou (c.1837-1892). When Jianhou was 80 years old, he was attacked from all sides by nine men. All nine were ineffective against Jianhou's defense. Each attacker was knocked away by a smooth series of blows and wardoffs.

When Yang Banhou's reputation also began to spread, he was challenged by a well known boxer named Liu. Hundreds, perhaps thousands, came to view the event. During their encounter, Liu grabbed Banhao's arm but his grip was easily countered, resulting in Liu's defeat. Yang Luchan complimented his son's success in combat, but explained that he had not yet reached the true artistic pinnacle of taijiquan. After all, Banhao's shirt sleeve was slightly torn in the contest.

Before Yang Luchan's sons became so formidable, they were forced into practice day and night under an almost reclusive spirit. Failures in learning their boxing lessons resulted in brow beatings at their father's hands. The psychological pressure was overwhelming for the sons. Banhao once tried to scale the family courtyard wall to freedom, but failed. His brother, Jianhou, was unsuccessful in a suicide attempt.

Compulsory studies alone did not make the Yang brothers superior boxers. Upon the death of their father, many friends, family members, and students gathered at Yang Luchan's graveside. A senior student with extraordinary boxing skills proclaimed himself the only worthy heir of the Yang Style Taijiquan. Chen Xiufeng had reason to claim this honor. First of all, he was no doubt better skilled than either of the Yang brothers. He was noted for possessing great internal energies for defeating any opponent, even without making physical contact. An example of this power is illustrated by his lifting a heavy wooden chair with the "sticking energy" of his palm. This formidable reputation served to intimidate the Yang brothers.

Yang Banhou and Yang Jianhou were inspired to study in earnest, with the help of their father's secret manuals. Afterwards, Jianhou was said to have attained the ability to levitate. So sensitive became his control over inner energy that a swallow could not take flight from his open palm. Such feats were not performed for amusement only. These abilities illustrate requirements for executing boxing techniques at the ultimate level of proficiency. Thus, both had finally reached a proficiency in the martial arts that their father had originally wished.

Chen Xiufeng later conceded the title back to the Yang brothers. He himself continued teaching in the Yencheng district of Henan Province. Mild-mannered Yang Jianhou attracted many students. His irritable brother, Banhou, chose only a small number of disciples. Because of this, his particular teachings eventually became extinct.

There are some interesting aspects of Yang Banhou's following. Being taught by his father and also a little by Wu Yuxiang, the found of the Wu style, Banhou passed on his acquired knowledge to a select few. One of his students was a farmer named Chang Qingling. Another Banhou student was a Manchurian whose Chinese name was Wu Quanyou (1834-1902). He was a dedicated student. After mastering the teachings of Banhou, Quanyou carefully imparted what he had learned to his son Wu Jianquan (1870-1942).

Wu Jianquan perfected the teachings of his father. His way of practicing taijiquan became known as the Wu Style. Sometimes his style and that of Wu Yuxiang's are differentiated by rendering their names into "Wu" and "Woo." In Chinese, both characters are written differently. For anyone who can read the Chinese, the names are easily distinguished. Wu Jianquan took his method to Shanghai. Later this Wu Style also became popular in Hong Kong and Singapore.

A student of Wu Jianquan became very well known, not particlarly for his martial art skills, but for his political standing. His name was Chu Minyi. Chu was the brother-in-law of Wang Qingwei, once President of China's Nationalist Government. Chu himself was ambassador to Japan after 1937.

Wu Jianquan's son-in-law, Ma Yuehliang, is likewise a teacher of the Wu Style. In Shanghai, Master Ma taught Sophia Delza, who taught in New York city at her own studio as well as at the United Nations. She wrote one of the first books in English dealing with taijiquan.

The above lineage stemming from Yang Banhou is only one branch of Yang Luchan's original style. The founder had other disciples. His student, Wu Hoqing, is said to have written a book of taijiquan but ascribed it to the earlier figure Wang Zongyue. Forging Wang's name on the taijiquan treatise helped make the book more popular.

Another student of Yang Luchan was Wang Lanting. Although Wang died at an early age, he possessed such great skills that he was a source of pride for his teacher. A student of Wang Lanting, Li Pinfu, illustrates the effectiveness of Wang's teachings. Li was once challenged by a qigong specialist. As his antagonist spoke, Li remained calm, petting a pet dog that he was holding in his arms. The impatient challenger darted forward only to be easily rebuffed by Li, who tenderly held onto his pet during the short scuffle.

The most influential line to descend from Yang Luchan was to pass on to his younger son, Yang Jianhou (1839-1917). Of pleasing disposition, Jienhou attracted many students. He was very proficient with weapons as well as the open-hand techniques. Two of his sons studied with him: Yang Shaohou (1862-1929) and Yang Chengfu (1883-1936).

Shaohou, the eldest son, began his study of taijiquan at the early age of seven. He learned much from his uncle Yang Banhou. In later years Shaohou became a superb boxer, but because of his rough manner most disciples studied with him for only a short time. According to rumor, he killed some of his opponents in boxing matches. The most important aspects of his art, characterized by small, compact movements, were imparted to very few. As a result, Yang Shaohou's particular style of taijiquan is very rare. He committed suicide in Nanjing in 1929, leaving only one son, Yang Chensheng.

Yang Jianhou had a second son, Chaohou, who died young and, therefore, did not perpetuate the Yang Style. The third son on the other hand, Yang Chengfu, had great influence. He systematized the style into the form so familiar today: natural postures utilizing steady, slow, expansive movements, executed with tensionless ease. Yang was never defeated even though most of his skill was self-taught. Beginning studies at age twenty, he was not very interested in taijiquan while his father lived. A genius in his own right, we can only imagine what accomplishments Yang Chengfu would have made if he had studied more diligently with his father.

The Yang Style was spread by Yang Chengfu from Beijing where he taught, to other areas of China, including Nanjing, Shanghai, Guangzhou and Hong Kong. Of Yang's four sons, it is Yang Zhenduo (born 1926, in Yongnian county, Hebei) who inherited the family system. Zhenduo has been very active in furthering interest in the art in China. He has also traveled overseas to share his special insights and knowledge. However, it is due to Yang Chengfu's senior disciples that the art was dispersed throughout the world. Part of his work includes a treatise on taijiquan called *Yang's Ten Important Points*.

Among the many students of Yang Chengfu are such well-known masters as Dong Yingjie (1888-1960) and Zheng Manqing (1900-1975). The first mentioned studied under Yang for close to twenty years, beginning at age seventeen. Dong taught in Hong Kong and his son, Dong Huling, taught in Hawaii.

It was in 1941 that taijiquan was first formally introduced in the United States under the instruction of Choy Hokpeng (1886-1957). Choy was also a student of Yang Chengfu. He started an institute in San Francisco which eventually had branches in Los Angeles and New York. His son, Choy Kamman, remains teaching in San Francisco. Another Yang Chengfu student also had great impact in the United States: Mr. Zheng Manqing.

Early in his career, Zheng Manqing was a professor living in Beijing. He began the study of taijiquan under Yang Chengfu's guidance in order to better his health which had deteriorated from tuberculosis. The taijiquan practice had a miraculous effect on his condition. As a result, his dedication to the art became a total commitment. After attaining a high level of boxing skills, Zheng traveled about China accepting and defeating a long line of challengers. On one occasion, while traveling through Sichuan Province, his talents were tested by a Daoist boxer surnamed Zou. Zheng was quickly defeated. This incident inspired Zheng to accept tutelage from this learned master. Zheng then altered some of the Yang style postures accordingly and his skill increased. As his techniques were perfected, his power became awesome.

Later, Zheng taught in Hunan, Taiwan and then in New York. Many of his students became noted masters of which the best known are living in Taiwan or in the United States. William C.C. Chen is one such student, now master, who originally came to New York with Zheng. Shi Shufeng, another senior student, chose to remain in Taiwan. At times, both Chen and Shi would illustrate their physical powers by letting students strike them anywhere on their bodies. Each time neither would suffer any ill effect.

Like many other sickly persons, Liang Dongcai (aka. T.T. Liang) sought Zheng Manqing's teachings with hopes that taijiquan would cure a physical ailment. In his case, it was a liver ailment. That was in 1950. Born in 1900, Liang continues to teach to this day.

Zheng Manqing had many other students that became well qualified instructors throughout the world. Zheng himself has stated that although the martial arts on mainland China have deteriorated to some degree during this century, there are still quite a few masters left to carry on their boxing traditions. Zheng believed that one of his own students, Zhang Zhigang, is among the most skilled of instructors on the mainland.

Today, taijiquan is truly international with representatives of various branches throughout the world. There remains a rich field of study for those interested in the extent of this influence. Hopefully future research will present in detail the state of this art as it exists in countries wherever it is represented.

19

CHART I: Old Chen Style Lineage

Others? ⋮ Qi Jiguang (1528-1587) Designed a routine consisting of 32 movements synthesized from 16 boxing styles.

Chen Wangting (1597-1644) Founder. c. 9th generation of Chen Pu clan. Designed seven different routines from 29 of the 32-movement routine learned from General Qi. One remains as the standard "Old Family Set" comprised of 74 forms.

- Chen Yuben (see Chart II)
- Chen Yuheng (see Chart II)
- Chen Bingqi
- Chen Pinjen

Chen Pingwang — Wang Zongyue (1736-1795) From Shanxi Province. Visited the Chen Village.

Chen Changxing 14th generation (1771-1853) Nicknamed "Mr. Name Board." First routine is the oldest form known; basis of later developments.

- Chen Hochai — Chen Hsi
- Li Pokui — Chen Wutian
- Yang Luchan (see — Chen Wuchang
- Charts III and IV)

Chen Gengyun 15th generation (died age 79). Son of Chen Changxing.

Chen Yenxi 16th generation (died age 81). Son of Chen Gengyun.

- Du Yuze 17th generation. (see Chart II)
- Wang Jiaxiang
- Tu Zongren
- Li Haochen
- Tsao Delin

Chen Fake 17th generation (1887-1957). Great grandson of Chen Changxing. Went to Beijiing in 1928. First to teach publicly.

- Chen Zhaopi Chen Fake's nephew.
- Gu Liuxin (1909-1990)
- Tien Xiuchen (died 1984).
- Chen Zhaoxu eldest — Chen Xiaoxing
- son of Chen Fake. younger brother
- Feng Zhiqiang (b. 1926). of Chen Xiaowang.
- Li Jianhua
- Pan Wingchou
- Many other students.

Chen Zhoquai 18th generation. Second son of Chen Fake.

- Feng Dabiao
- Zhang Chundong
- Chen Chinghong
- Ma Hong

Chen Xiaowang 18th generation (born 1946). Eldest son of Chen Zhaoxu. Main representative of the Chen Family Taijiquan. Developed a simplified 38-movement set.

CHART II: New Chen Style Lineage & Others

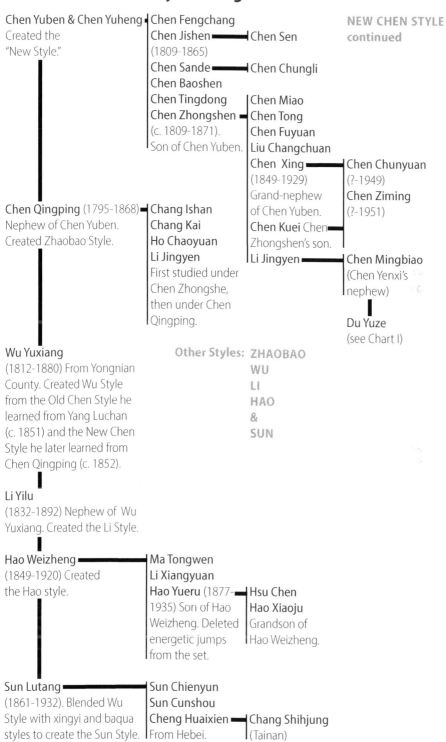

Chen Yuben & Chen Yuheng
Created the
"New Style."

Chen Fengchang
Chen Jishen ━━━ Chen Sen
(1809-1865)
Chen Sande ━━━ Chen Chungli
Chen Baoshen
Chen Tingdong   Chen Miao
Chen Zhongshen ◄ Chen Tong
(c. 1809-1871).   Chen Fuyuan
Son of Chen Yuben. Liu Changchuan

NEW CHEN STYLE
continued

Chen Xing ━━━ Chen Chunyuan
(1849-1929)   (?-1949)
Grand-nephew   Chen Ziming
of Chen Yuben.   (?-1951)

Chen Qingping (1795-1868) ◄ Chang Ishan
Nephew of Chen Yuben.   Chang Kai
Created Zhaobao Style.   Ho Chaoyuan
                              Li Jingyen
                              First studied under
                              Chen Zhongshe,
                              then under Chen
                              Qingping.

Chen Kuei Chen ━
Zhongshen's son.

Li Jingyen ━━━ Chen Mingbiao
                    (Chen Yenxi's
                    nephew)

Du Yuze
(see Chart I)

Wu Yuxiang
(1812-1880) From Yongnian
County. Created Wu Style
from the Old Chen Style he
learned from Yang Luchan
(c. 1851) and the New Chen
Style he later learned from
Chen Qingping (c. 1852).

Other Styles: ZHAOBAO
WU
LI
HAO
&
SUN

Li Yilu
(1832-1892) Nephew of Wu
Yuxiang. Created the Li Style.

Hao Weizheng ━━━ Ma Tongwen
(1849-1920) Created   Li Xiangyuan
the Hao style.   Hao Yueru (1877- ━ Hsu Chen
                        1935) Son of Hao   Hao Xiaoju
                        Weizheng. Deleted Grandson of
                        energetic jumps   Hao Weizheng.
                        from the set.

Sun Lutang ━━━ Sun Chienyun
(1861-1932). Blended Wu   Sun Cunshou
Style with xingyi and baqua Cheng Huaixien ━ Chang Shihjung
styles to create the Sun Style. From Hebei.   (Tainan)

CHART III: Yang Style Lineage

Yang Luchan (1799-1872). Native of Yongnian County, Hebei; taught in Beijig. Nicknamed "Yang the Invincible." Modified the Old Chen Style to better suit goals of health. Founder of the Yang Style.

- Chen Hsiufeng
- Wu Hoqing
- Li Ruidong
- **Wang Lanting** ────── **Li Pinfu**
- **Wan Chun** (Manchu Nobles' Athletic Camp)
- **Ling Shan** (Manchu Nobles' Athletic Camp)
- **Wu Yuxiang** (1812-1880). (see Chart II)
- **Quan You** (see Chart IV)
- **Yang Banhou** (1837-1892). Second son of Yang Luchan. (see Chart IV)

Yang Jianhou (1839-1917). Third son of Yang Luchan. Further modified the form from his father into the "middle style".

- Chi De
- **Xu Yusheng** (1879-1945)
- Yang Chaoyuan
- **Yang Shaohou** (1862-1929) ────── Yang Chensheng
- First son of Yang Jienhou. ────── Tian Shaoxian

Yang Chengfu (1883-1936). Third son of Yang Jienhou. Great influence in spreading the art to many parts of China. Standardized the form of taijiquan with graceful, extended movements, known as the "Big Style." It became the most popular style.

- **Dong Yingjie** Studied under Yang Chengfu. ────── **Jasmine Dong** (Hong Kong). Daughter of Dong Yingjie.
- **Fu Zhongwen** Nephew of Yang Chengfu. **Dong Huling** (Hawaii). Son of Dong Yingjie.
- **Yang Shouchung** (Hong Kong). (b. 1909). Eldest son of Yang Chengfu. **Li Huangtse** (Shanghai)
- **Yang Zhenji** (Handan, Hebei). Second son of Yang Chengfu. **Huang Wenshan** (Los Angeles)
- **Yang Zhenguo** (Handan, Hebei). Fourth son of Yang Chengfu.
- **Chen Weiming** ────── **Liang Chingyu** (Hong Kong). Chief disciple
- **Li Yahsuan** of Chen Weiming.
- **Wu Huichun** (?-1937).
- **Wan Lating** (died young).
- **Choy Hok-peng** (1886-1957). ────── Choy Kamman
- **Zheng Manqing** (1900-1975). ──────
- Many other students. **Liang Tungtsai** (born 1900).

Yang Zhenduo (Taiyua, Hebei). Third son of Yang Chengfu, born in 1926. Most of training was under his brothers, Shaouchung and Zhenji.

- **Yang Jun** (Taiyua, Hebei). Grandson of Yang Zhenduo.
- **William C.C. Chen**
- **Chang Chihkang**
- **Shi Shufeng**
- **Huang Shenghsien** (Singapore).
- Many other students.

22

CHART IV: Yang and Wu Style Lineages

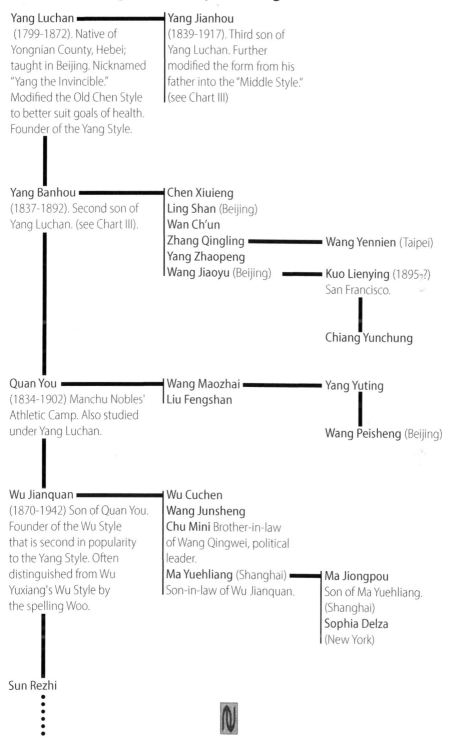

Yang Luchan ▬▬▬▬
(1799-1872). Native of
Yongnian County, Hebei;
taught in Beijing. Nicknamed
"Yang the Invincible."
Modified the Old Chen Style
to better suit goals of health.
Founder of the Yang Style.

Yang Jianhou
(1839-1917). Third son of
Yang Luchan. Further
modified the form from his
father into the "Middle Style."
(see Chart III)

Yang Banhou ▬▬▬▬
(1837-1892). Second son of
Yang Luchan. (see Chart III).

Chen Xiuieng
Ling Shan (Beijing)
Wan Ch'un
Zhang Qingling ▬▬▬▬ **Wang Yennien** (Taipei)
Yang Zhaopeng
Wang Jiaoyu (Beijing) ▬▬▬▬ **Kuo Lienying** (1895-?)
San Francisco.

Chiang Yunchung

Quan You ▬▬▬▬
(1834-1902) Manchu Nobles'
Athletic Camp. Also studied
under Yang Luchan.

Wang Maozhai ▬▬▬▬ **Yang Yuting**
Liu Fengshan

Wang Peisheng (Beijing)

Wu Jianquan ▬▬▬▬
(1870-1942) Son of Quan You.
Founder of the Wu Style
that is second in popularity
to the Yang Style. Often
distinguished from Wu
Yuxiang's Wu Style by
the spelling Woo.

Wu Cuchen
Wang Junsheng
Chu Mini Brother-in-law
of Wang Qingwei, political
leader.
Ma Yuehliang (Shanghai) ▬▬▬▬ **Ma Jiongpou**
Son-in-law of Wu Jianquan. Son of Ma Yuehliang.
(Shanghai)
Sophia Delza
(New York)

Sun Rezhi

23

References — Books

Chen, Yearning K. *T'ai Chi Ch'uan – Its Effects and Practical Applications.* Translated by Kuo-shui Chang. Shanghai: Kelly and Walsh, Ltd. 1947.

Chen, Xiaowang, editor. *Chen Style 38 Ways Taijiquan.* [In Chinese] Hong Kong: Ke Science Popularization Publishing Co., Guangzhou Division, 1987.

Cheng, Man-ch'ing and R. W. Smith. *T'ai Chi.* Rutland, VT: Charles E. Tuttle Co., 1973.

Delza, Sophia. *Tai Chi Ch'uan-Body and Mind in Harmony.* Albany: State University of New York Press, revised edition 1985.

Draeger, D. and R. Smith. *Asian Fighting Arts.* New York: Berkeley Medallion Books, 1974.

Gu, Liuxin, editor. *Pao Chuei: Chen Style Taijiquan,* 2nd Routine. [In Chinese] Hong Kong: Hai Feng Publishing Co. 1985; 1986 second printing.

Gu, Liuxin, with Zhiqiang Feng, Dabiao Feng and Xiaowang Chen. *Chen Style Taijiquan.* Hong Kong: Hai Feng Publishing Co., in conjunction with Beijing: Zhaohua Publishing House, 1984.

Horwitz, T., and S. Kimmelman with H. H. Lui. *Tai Chi Ch'uan: The Technique of Power.* Chicago: Chicago Review Press, 1976.

Huang, Wen-shan. *Fundamentals of Tai Chi Ch'uan.* Hong Kong: South Sky Book Co., 1979.

Jou, Tsung Hwa. *The Tao of Tai-Chi Chuan – Way to Rejuvenation.* Warwick, NY: Tai Chi Foundation, 1981.

Liang, T.T. *T'ai Chi Ch'uan for Health and Self-Defense – Philosophy and Practice.* New York: Vintage Books, 1977.

Lo, Benjamin Pang Jen and M. Inn, R. Amacker and S. Foe. *The Essence of T'ai Chi Ch'uan – The Literary Tradition.* Richmond, CA: North Atlantic Books, 1979.

Luo Hung-yuan and Gu Dai-chuan. *Taijiquan: Principles and Training.* [In Chinese] Guandong High Level Education Publication Co., 1988.

Shen Jiajen, editor et al. *Chen Family Taijiquan.* [In Chinese] Hong Kong: Hsin Wen Bookstore Publishing Co. No date.

Smith, R. *Chinese Boxing – Masters and Methods.* Tokyo: Kodansha International, Ltd., 1974.

Soong, Tien Lung-jir. *Secret Chen Family Taijiquan Introduction.* [In Chinese] I Chuen Bookstore, Taipei, 1983.

Su, Kun-ming, editor. *Subtleties of the Chen Style Old Form of Taijiquan.* [In Chinese] Taipei: Hua-lien Hua-lien Publishing Co., 1974.

Wile, D., compiled and translated. *T'ai-chi Touchstones — Yang Family Secret Transmissions.* Brooklyn, NY: Sweet Ch'i Press, 1983.

Yang Jwing-ming. *Advanced Yang Style Tai Chi Chuan, Vol. I*, Boston: Yang's Martial Arts Academy, 1986.

References — Articles

Bu Xieming, "Birthplace of Taijiquan Boxing," In Land Where Martial Arts Began (6), Beijing: *China Reconstructs* (1983), p. 26-30.

Chen, Gene Ching Hong. "Chen Style Tai Chi: The 'Real' Tai Chi Chuan?" *Inside Kung-Fu*, Vol. 9, No. 11 (Nov 1982), p. 73-76.

Chen, Gene Ching Hong with T. Chan & R. Judice. "Power Without Pride: The Ethical Grandmaster of Chen Tai Chi," *Inside Kung-Fu*, Vol. 2, No.7 (July 1984), p.63-65.

Hefter, L. "Chen Style Tai Chi Chuan," *Inside Kung-Fu*, Vol. 9, No. 6 (June 1982), p.36-41.

Kan, Guixang, "A Brief History of Chen Style Tai Chi Chuan," Anthony Chan and Diana Hong, translators. *Inside Kung-Fu*, Vol. 9, No. 6 (June 1982), p. 41.

Meehan, J. "The Combat Secrets of Chen Tai Chi," *Inside Kung-Fu*, Vol. 11, No. 8 (Aug 1984), p. 69-73.

Miller, R., "Chen Style Tai Chi," *Black Belt*, Vol. 20, No. 4 (April 1982), p. 46-48.

Seidel, A. "A Taoist Immortal of the Ming Dynasty: Chang San-feng," In *Self and Society in Ming Thought*, W. T. deBary, editor. New York: Columbia University Press (1970), p. 483-531.

Stubenbaum, D. "Chen Tai Chi Chuan: Innerer Kreis der Geheimnisse," [In German] *Karate Budo Journal*, No. 5 (May 1990), p. 54-56.

2

The Presence of the Eyes in the Action of Taijiquan
by Sophia Delza

Photos by Lisa Leviki. Drawings by Ray Copper.

In taking the Basic Position at the start of taijiquan, the stance, torso, spine, shoulder, hand and head positions should be given particular attention. So should the eyes. That we lose track of them during the action, especially in the early learning process, is readily "forgivable." The subtlety of the eye-muscle movement and the necessity of the mind's presence behind the eye-action need not be emphasized until that time when the taijiquan player is prepared, physically and mentally, to experience many of the subtler aspects of the exercise: the smooth balance of the continuous motion, the physiological correctness of the forms, the space-tempo relationships, awareness of stillness in action, as well as the ability to function "intrinsically," i.e., without false effort. An unmistakable look will itself develop when one feels the harmony of what is being done. Eyes will be alert, calm, knowing and poised.

I have, in various essays, given thought to the various structural elements of taijiquan from the point of view of physiology and philosophy. I have closely examined the subtleties in taijiquan's weaving forms and patterns; I have pictured the ever moving yin-yang elements in "The Life of the Hand." Now I venture to analyze more or less scientifically what happens in and to the eyes in a physical way during the active variations of movement.

Just as the physical body acquires a spirit in doing taijiquan, so the eyes (or the mind's eye) become and remain alert, peaceful and contained. The eyes can never be vacuous in taijiquan, nor will they portray anxiety or worry even while one is trying to remember and coordinate, though the eyes can, as we know, radiate any emotion: from hate to love plus all the emotions in between. The spirit of the movement in taijiquan seeps through the whole physical being. Therefore, the eyes—regardless of the physical changes occurring—will feel light, secure, and impersonal. All of this is brought about naturally, not solely by emotional means, but through one's complete physical being.

The regulation of eye movements is as clearly organized in the structure of taijiquan as is the play of every part of the body—large or small—contributing to physical and mental harmony.

The eyes seem to be so quietly set and unmoving during the activity that they are oftentimes outside of one's notice—both the performer's and the observer's. Should the eyes, however, shift randomly or dartingly, the overall impression would be one of nervousness, uncertainty or restlessness.

Eye movements are unnoticed not because there is so much to do and/or observe in the ever-changing patterns of the exercise, but because they are focussing quietly and being instinctively controlled by the smooth consistency required of all taijiquan movement changes.

The word "eyes," as used here, refers to all aspects of their physical composition—eyelids, eyeballs and the muscles (which control the eye's ability to focus far or near, upward, downward, sideways or obliquely)—as well as emotions which can affect their appearance.

In the action of taijiquan, all motion is intrinsically balanced, where form creates the continual variations of yin-yang dynamics, where extremes of tension are never required or permitted, and so it is with the use of the eyes, which respond intrinsically to the necessity of the movement at the moment. Superfluous effort of any kind is not needed to regulate or stimulate the eyes, nor is it ever part of the action of the eyes, such as lowering the eye to look straight down at the body nor raising the lids to see far upward at a 180-degree angle. Both movements are extreme.

Eye muscles are gently manipulated, always in basic slow tempo, adjusted to move or not to move with the body, responding to form, pattern, space and direction, unless otherwise directed by the requirement of the particular position of the body and head. (This is explained later.) As indicated, the eyes behave in an organically instinctive and intrinsic way, in accord with the nature of taijiquan, which is termed a "soft-intrinsic" system of activating the body for physical, emotional and mental well-being.

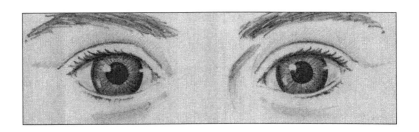

The eyes are the cottage of the spirit.

– *Chinese proverb*

It is more difficult to experience the "soft-intrinsic" variation in the play of than it is, obviously, to feel the dynamic changes in the constantly manipulated body forms. Just as physical action is not animated by an extrinsic force, so the eyes similarly maintain a calm, "impersonal" and therefore natural ease. When frowning, peering, straining, and otherwise expressing strong emotions do not disrupt intrinsic integrity and equilibrium, then the total being can achieve, through taijiquan's harmonious principles, health and superior awareness.

The Basic Eye Position

The way the head is held at all times (with a few exceptions) affects the basic eye position. The head must be held erect, upright, so that the crown of the head is directed upward vertically as if attached by a "silken cord to the heavens." The chin, therefore, is not pressed inward toward the neck, nor is it tilted upward. The shoulders are low and relaxed, and the neck light. The mouth remains closed with the tip of the tongue lightly resting against the upper palate. With this perfect carriage of the head, the eyes will experience subtle muscular activity but outwardly will appear unchanged.

The overall eye position from which the dynamic variations occur is determined by the way the lids are held or moved. The gaze, in the basic eye position, is lowered to a 45-degree angle. (When the eyes are wide open and look directly forward, the gaze is at a 90-degree angle.) The eyes, with the gaze at a 45-degree angle, can see out at a long diagonal, downward path and come to rest on the ground approximately ten or twelve feet from where one is poised. Eye muscles will feel light and untaxed. They are in a "neutral" position.

The eyes maintain a gaze of 45-degrees 90% of the time during the exercise. We know that without effort the ears hear. So too, the eyes can see without any effort.

FEATURES OF EYE-BEHAVIOR*

*All explanations and illustrations are based on the Wu system of taijiquan.

The Basic Eye Position as illustrated in the Beginning form of taijiquan.

Following the Taiji Beginning Form, the body shifts its weight right and the knees bend. The eyes continue looking out on a long diagonal path with the gaze at a 45° angle.

I. The Quiet Unmoving Eyes: when eyelids, eyeballs and muscles are not activated and remain downward in the basic 45-degree gazing position.

    a) In a position where the body does not move out of place during a series of arm/leg movements, the eyes will be "fixed," looking downward at a 45-degree angle, focusing on an unspecific area on the ground. This is "pure" stillness of the quiet eye.

    b) When the knees bend and the figure remains in the same space, the eyes do not change, but simply see a different area, slightly nearer than when the legs are straight. This, too, is "pure" stillness of the eyes.

c) When the entire figure turns, let us say, to the right side, if the body level remains the same, the eyes will simply see another area, without any eye-muscle movement. The gaze is quietly set and remains lowered 45 degrees during the movement.

d) When the movement is such that the entire figure moves forward or backward, as in Brush-Knee-Twist (Walking-Step Form), the eyes do not stir. One sees different areas on the ground farther forward as one advances, farther backward as one retreats. The path of vision remains still.

Brush Knee-Twist Step Form. The eyes see out on a long diagonal path and the gaze is at a 45° angle. Note: Between the stages of stillness are moments of eye activity necessary when executing the different forms.

The above illustrations emphasize the fact that the eyes and the unchanging muscles have remained still, quiet, and light. Such conscious control helps to create calmness.

II. The Quiet Moving Eyes: muscles react with changes in body positions.

a) In the Hand Strums the Lute Form, a hand moves into the basic line of vision, thus "forcing" an eye-muscle reaction. In the following illustration, the figure has taken a Walking Stance, with the right arm placed outward shoulder high. The eyes are free to gaze along the basic 45-degree path. The figure then sits back into an Empty Step Form, at the same time bringing the right hand to center, in front of the nose and chin, blocking the line of vision. The eyes are then "forced" to see the tops of the fingers; this activates the eye-muscles. When the hand is removed, the eyes refocus. But "interference" in the line of vision automatically activates the muscles to become tense.

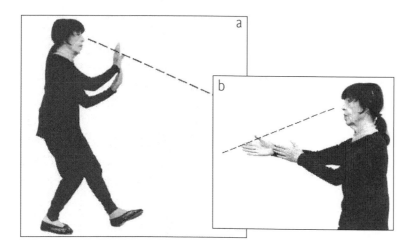

Left: **Hand Strums the Lute.** The eyes are in the basic 45° angle gaze as the right fingertips enter the field of vision causing the eyes to refocus.

Right: **Grasping the Bird's Tail.** The eyes see out on a long diagonal path. The view is interrupted by the placement of the hands as in Hand Strums the Lute. Therefore, the eyes see the thumb of the right hand.

b) The eye action in the Hands Strum the Lute form occurs frequently with variations, more or less tensed depending on the form. For example, in the Wu Style's third series, when a leg is outstretched and an arm is extended shoulder high with the head turned toward it, the eyes have a "longer look" and are focused on the thumb of that hand; thus the tension in the eye muscles is lessened. The eye muscles are often stirred by a variety of movements. Eyes are less tense when looking at an object which is far away than when seeing one that is close. The eye muscles are never over-worked in taijiquan since no positions are repeated successively.

c) When the torso sinks or bends forward or sideways and the head and neck remain still, the eyes will, therefore, see the ground closer to the feet, thus activating the eye-muscles, as illustrated above in *a* and *b*. The gaze will remain at a 45-degree angle.

In all the above illustrations, the look has remained unaltered—quiet and calm; the feeling of stillness predominates. All the action, light or strong, is intrinsic, i.e., done according to the physiological laws of nature.

31

III. The Active (Willed) Eye Movements: the eyes are directed to bestir themselves in coordination with certain movements and forms.

a) For Wu Style Cloud-Arms Form. At certain times the eyes move from a 45-degree gaze to an open-eyed 90-degree gaze in the following way. The eyes look to the right at the palm of the left hand which is placed near the out-stretched right arm; the left hand is then moved toward the face, the palm as high as the eyes and about ten to twelve inches away. This eye-level position raises the gaze to a 90-degree angle. Throughout this form, the eye muscles are being activated both to "rest" by returning the eyes to the 45-degree gaze, and to be stirred to a 90-degree gaze and finally to allow the eyes to look far into the distance, thus resting the eyes fully. Such changes, by being consciously directed, extend the range of eye exercise movements.

Cloud Arms Form. The eyes see the palm of the left hand, which is held about twelve inches away from the face. The eyes are opened wide in a 90° gaze.

b) In the Fying Oblique Form, the body position is held unchanged as the right foot, right hand and head are moved. The head is tipped downward slightly toward the right side. The eyes look down obliquely at the upturned right palm which is in front of the right knee. Throughout this complex moving form, the head and eyes hold their position in respect to the right hand, while the torso is regulated to release pressure in the neck. The form ends with the eyes seeing the back of the right hand, the head still slightly tipped. The eyes and head then gently recover the normal position on the next transition movement. There are several transition movements in which the head is tipped to exercise the muscles in a different and more intense way.

Left: *Transition to Flying Oblique Form.* The head is slightly tucked. The eyes see the right wrist.

Right: *Single Whip Form.* Occurs nine times in the Wu Style. The eyes experience a variety of dynamic changes during this form.

c) The Single Whip Form appears nine times in the Wu Style. The eyes experience a variety of dynamic changes which are specially designed for this form. The eyes follow the movement of the left hand, which goes at shoulder height from the right side to the left side. The eyes follow the path of the hand as it rises and falls. The eye muscles change in slow succession from a relaxed to a tensed state and back to a relaxed state. In passing from the right to the left side, the hand travels in a parabola. The eyes are then activated more tensely as the palm reaches the center of the curve at chest level because the gaze has moved in a downward and inward path. The gaze then moves upward toward the left, re-leasing eye pressure as the hand completes the movement at the left side, still at shoulder height. Here the eyes see the back of the hand. The eyes have been slowly activated by a relatively light tension and a strong one, and then "released" to become quietly and evenly relaxed at the end of the arm-hand-head movement. (The head is not tipped downward as it moves from the right side to the left while the eyes follow the hand.)

d) The Oblique Look: When the eyes are directed to look far right or left, the head must be slightly tipped downward to avoid extreme pressure on the muscles (as in the Flying Oblique Form explained above). In a transition between the Single Whip and the En-folding Form, the head is tipped to the left side and then moves to off-center right to look obliquely at the right upturned palm which is at far right.

This eye position appears only once, perhaps because it is most tense. The eyes recover their neutral position on the next movement and, relatively speaking, have a "rest" in the basic 45-degree gaze.

Transition from the
Single Whip Form
to the Enfolding Form.

• • •

Suffice it to say that the subtle or obvious eye changes stimulate the agility and the power of the eyes, the movements of which are as necessary to nurture "health and awareness" as are all the other more easily discerned bodily manoeuver.

This analysis encompasses the range of the movements and "stillnesses" of the eye-action: seeing and looking and not commenting or mentally reacting to what is observed. The eyes function as naturally as does every other part of the body, according to the dictates of the mind and the demands of form, direction, space, time and the dynamic interplay of all these factors.

The eyes become (and remain) intelligent and tranquil and maintain the expressive spirit of the individual personality. They express the essence of taijiquan: calmness, containment, and the comprehension of some possible potential development of consciousness. The Chinese say the eyes are the "cottage of the spirit," the glow of the spirit of equanimity. S. E. Cirlot, in the *Dictionary of Symbols*, says:

Light is

symbolic of

intelligence and of the spirit.

. . . the process of seeing

represents a spiritual act and

symbolizes understanding.

Delza, Sophia. (1992, #71). The life of the hand: Its significance in t'ai-chi ch'uan. *Fighting Arts International*, 31-33.

3

Taijiquan — Learning How to Learn
by Linda Lehrhaupt, Ph.D.

Left: Yang Qingyu demonstrating a Yang-style in Puli, Taiwan. Center: Paolo D'Annibala, a Yang-style practitioner, Rome. Right: Tu Zongren practicing a Chen Style, Taipei. Photos courtesy of M. DeMarco, P. D'Annibale, and Z.R. Tu.

Introduction

When I first began to study taijiquan in 1978, I was attracted to it, like many beginning students, by its description as a form of "meditation in motion." I had visions of flowing in dream-like movements, sensing peace and harmony all around me. I arrived at my first class full of happy expectations, sure that I was about to experience the secret of the Daoist masters. As I watched my teacher move with elegance and gentle power, I became even more excited. That excitement soon turned into frustration and disappointment as I struggled to learn the two short movements she so patiently repeated. At the end of the class, I was sure of only one thing: either my expectations had to go out the door or I did. I chose to stay.

Over and over during the past ten years that I have been teaching, I watch my own students arrive at their first class with the same expectations that I had. They seek to be more peaceful, to find balance, to learn something that will help them cope with stress. Their longing is so great that many hope to reap the benefits of taijiquan from the moment they begin to learn the form. In this mode of wishful thinking and longing for Paradise Now, they often ignore common sense. No one would expect to be a great pianist after one lesson, and yet many beginning taiji students believe that after one short class they will be able to move with the grace and effortlessness of an experienced taiji practitioner.

Most taiji students who stop studying after a short time do so, not because taiji is difficult to learn, but because their expectations are not satisfied quickly enough. The ensuing frustration is so emotionally painful they decide to quit rather than continue to be disappointed.

> **When the emphasis**
> **is on how and**
> **not simply what is learned,**
> **a student embraces everything**
> **as part of his taiji practice,**
> **including his feelings and expectations.**

Part of the problem lies in the fact that students approach learning taiji as something to achieve, something to be successful at. But learning taiji, especially in the beginning, is really a process of learning how to learn. Learning how to learn means that what a student discovers about himself is just as important, if not more so, than simply performing a taiji movement correctly. When the emphasis is on how and not simply what is learned, a student embraces everything as part of his taiji practice, including his feelings and expectations. Frustrations, disappointment, or low self-esteem, instead of becoming obstacles to practice, can be transformed into fertile ground for learning about oneself.

In learning how to learn, we discover the essence of taiji as a meditative practice: the study of the self. Here, too, students must often re-examine their expectations of what meditation is. Many think it is the path to an enlightened state of bliss and wisdom, a state in which we are above all problems, free from attachment and desire. But the study of the self is, in fact, the study of the self as it is, not just the narrow view of how we would like ourselves to be. Practicing taiji as meditation invites us to stay open to each moment exactly as it is, to remain present and acknowledge all of our experience, not selecting or rejecting anything. By staying open we create space to examine our fears, disappointments, and expectations. Bringing them into awareness allows us to work with them in a healing way. Their power to control us lessens because they no longer remain hidden.

Practicing taiji as meditation, the heart of which is learning how to learn, requires that we cultivate six qualities to support our practice. In the discussion that follows, I would like to examine each of them as they relate to the study of taijiquan.

Left: A posture from a taijiquan sword form. Weapons training is a vital aspect of deepening a student's understanding of the taiji principles. Right: The characteristics of water—its flow, softness and ability to accommodate to any shape—are qualities taiji practitioners seek to emulate. Photos courtesy of L. Lehrhaupt.

Effort

Perhaps the most important part of making an effort is taking responsibility for our learning rather than expecting someone else to do our work for us. Though we all would agree that "from nothing comes nothing," we often secretly hope that we can learn something without having to work at it. If we don't learn something, we are quick to blame the teacher or the method rather than examine our own commitment in terms of time and energy.

If there is one hard cold fact about taijiquan, it is that without regular practice we do not progress. We can talk about developing balance or coordination a hundred times, but it will never replace one training session. Developing a consistent practice schedule is not easy; there is so much in our private or work lives that seems to demand our attention. Yet when we don't practice we set ourselves up for a cycle of disappointment: we don't develop because we don't practice; we don't practice because we don't seem to develop.

When we begin to feel uneasy about how little we practice, we have an excellent opportunity to study ourselves. There can be many different reasons not to practice: we are afraid of not doing it right, we do not feel calm enough, we find it difficult to be alone with ourselves, we feel we are wasting time. Making an effort in this case implies letting these feelings arise and acknowledging them. In doing so, their power to overwhelm or paralyze us lessens, and we can renew our commitment to do it again one more time. We may do this many times, but each time we are getting to know ourselves a bit better. Practicing is something that needs to be practiced. When we give ourselves the chance, the motivation and sense of flow often help us to continue. If we do not choose to continue, then our choice is the result of a conscious decision resulting from the effort to study ourselves.

I have purposely avoided the word *discipline* because I feel we confuse the word *effort* with *discipline*. Discipline often implies forcing ourselves to do something, whatever we feel. Discipline is something we measure in terms of time and amount: the more the better. It often involves ignoring where we are in service to achieving a future goal. Top athletes are said to be disciplined: that many succumb to doping or other unhealthy practices in pushing their bodies beyond human limits is the negative side of this do-or-die attitude to training.

When applied to taijiquan, this kind of discipline hinders rather than furthers practice. We no longer pay attention to our feelings or working with ourselves, but emphasize meeting a standard. It is taiji without heart.

Focus

Learning how to learn requires that we develop the capacity to quiet the mind so that we can focus on the work at hand. To quiet the mind does not mean to erase thought, but to dampen and subdue the internal dialogue that occupies so much mental energy. It also does not mean to control thought, but to experience a sense of opening and spaciousness that happens when we are no longer the prisoner of our thoughts and emotions. Mental space is created when we begin to see our thoughts for what they are—just thoughts, and we stop identifying with them as representing who and all we really are.

Simple, clear exercises in which the thinking mind is given a task are the most effective techniques for channeling scattered mental energy into a clear line of focus. Learning a taiji form, which involves repeating each movement over and over, is an excellent practice in this respect. True, not all students experience learning a move as a simple clear task, but when they have the chance to practice over and over, encouraged by a concentrated class environment, their minds have a chance to focus and quiet down. During training they have an opportunity to set aside their mental preoccupation with themselves or with other problems and concentrate on the task at hand. Such concentration, while tiring, can also be rejuvenating and therapeutic.

In taijiquan we have a wonderful opportunity to develop focus—a fine-tuned, laser-sharp concentration that is enhanced by practicing the form and paying attention. Each time we are dreaming, we return to the feeling of muscles and joints moving, the body in motion. It is partly for this reason that learning or teaching a form quickly robs the student of the opportunity to work with precision. Learning a form quickly becomes a rush to get something and display it, rather than experiencing the subtle process of fine-tuning a movement. It leads to a lot of messy, dreamy or even technically competent taiji, but not one that emphasizes the inner development of the practitioner.

Awareness

Joseph Goldstein, a teacher of Vipassana, or insight meditation, describes awareness as "bare attention," which "means observing things as they are, without choosing, without comparing, without evaluating, without laying our projections and expectations onto what is happening, cultivating instead a choiceless and non-interfering awareness" (Goldstein, 1987: 20).

In taiji practice, maintaining bare attention applies to the state of mind in which we learn and teach a movement. For the teacher, it means to emphasize the experience of doing a movement, not demanding millimeter exactness and conformity to some fixed image of the taiji posture. Often the minutely precise corrections that some taiji teachers make are a substitute for good teaching, which involves working with each student personally, where he is at in the moment, rather than simply treating him as clay that can be molded into a dead shape.

Maintaining bare attention for the student means to attempt to be fully present in each moment, to be awake, aware, and able to move and respond to change without resistance. In taiji it means to be here and now when doing the form, not dancing in Dreamland. Moment by moment we experience our body, movement, environment separately and as one. It is the unity and uniqueness of each movement/moment that we experience as the taiji.

Patience

I often tell my beginning students that there is one phrase they are going to hear over and over again until they think that is all I know how to say. That phrase is, "Once More!" Patience in taiji practice is exercising faith and making a commitment to the learning process of "Once More." What is this process exactly? When we do a movement again and again, our practice is open-ended. Repeating something is not a mechanical re-run of an activity or a determined

40

effort to do something solely to get it right, but a path of discovery. We pay attention to each moment, to experience what we can learn in that moment. It may be something concrete, such as noticing we are not in balance when we take a step, or it may be the joy of experiencing coordinated movement, where effort and flow merge in seamless non-action: doing without doing.

Shunryu Suzuki Roshi, a Zen Master, calls this quality of a discovering mind "beginner's mind." When something is new for us, we are generally open and ready to receive, eager to experience all aspects. When we think we have mastered something, we close down to seeing new perspectives because we've made an investment in knowing. We don't want to risk or challenge this feeling of security. When we lose patience and do not want to try again, we are closing down to life and to learning from our own experience. As Suzuki Roshi writes:

> In the beginner's mind there are many possibilities;
> in the expert's mind there are few. – Suzuki 1982: 21

Perhaps the most difficult part of repeating something over and over again is learning to work with boredom. In fact the moment when one is bored is the moment when a deeper level of learning can take place. What we label as boredom is often a simple name that covers much deeper feelings that we do not want to acknowledge: frustration with the difficulty of learning, disappointment at what we label as our own clumsiness, anger at not being quicker to achieve something. Far from being a state of deadness, boredom is a rich field for studying the self and a door to experiencing the preciousness of each moment. It's then that we can go beyond simple mastery or getting a move right and be one with each moment by being awake and aware, with all that is part of it. Being committed to "Once More," to making a gentle resolve to start again in each moment, is the heart of this process.

Gentleness

We often approach learning taiji with a harsh, self-critical attitude that does not allow us to be either patient or gentle with ourselves. We apply the same competitive spirit that is so valued in our world, which leads us to judge ourselves constantly, to set up standards of discipline that are personally difficult to attain, or to emphasize our way as the better one. Perna Chodron, a Tibetan Buddhist nun and student of Chogyam Trungpa, Rinpoche, writes: "Meditation practice isn't about trying to throw ourselves away and become

41

something better. It's about befriending who we already are" (Chodron 1991: 4). If we are to experience taiji practice in the same way—as a continual process of opening to ourselves—then we need to let go of these destructive ideas and practice making friends with ourselves. It is a gentle process of acknowledging our strengths without pride and recognizing our weaknesses without scorn. We try to work with ourselves in the same way we would help a baby stand up after he had fallen down. A sense of humor is very helpful in learning to practice gentleness.

Taijiquan practitioners practicing push-hands in a park in Taipei, Taiwan.
Photo courtesy of L. Lehrhaupt.

Letting Go

Pema Chodron writes: "The quality of opening or letting go ... helps us to rediscover this ability that we already have to open beyond small-mindedness and to let go of any kind of fixation or limited view.... But letting go is not so easy. Rather it's something that happens as a result of working with precision and gentleness. In other words, as you work with being really faithful to the technique in our case, taijiquan, and being as precise as you can and simultaneously as kind as you can, the ability to let go seems to happen to you. The discovery of your ability to let go spontaneously arises; you don't force it" (Chodron 1991: 19).

Letting go of the desire to develop special powers is an important step in taiji practice. There is, unfortunately, a tendency to promote the development of special powers or heightened faculties by teachers and students of taiji and qigong. In one form, it involves repeating stories of famous masters who were said to have such powers as throwing people without touching them, or being able to use such powers to bend steel or withstand physical attack

42

without injury. Others talk about mastering qi power and emphasize either its martial arts applications or secret healing techniques. There are investigations of such stories, especially in the sciences of psychology and anthropology, and this is not the place to enter into a discussion of whether these reports are true or not. The real problem for students is a spiritual one: seeking extraordinary powers is a misuse of sacred tradition and feeds our ego and need to master others rather than mastering the self.

The most beneficial way to work with the desire to be special is to acknowledge it. Secretly holding onto the wish to be special but denying that we feel this way is a great obstacle to knowing and making friends with ourselves. We all long to be special in some way so that we can feel better about ourselves. When we name it for what it is, we practice being transparent and take the first important step in letting go of the need to be better than others.

In taiji we also experience the difficulty of letting go in learning to relax while doing the form and in practicing push-hands. Letting go in the form means maintaining posture without force, recognizing bad habits, opening to emotional or physical traumas that manifest as unhealthy or stuck body postures—and most of all feeling joy in movement, even if it's clumsy.

Learning to relax in a taiji posture is the most difficult aspect for many taiji students. As a teacher, one often stands before a student whose shoulders are up around his ears as he holds his arms outstretched at chest height, only to be told, "But I am relaxed!" The flood of relief that fills the student's face as he lowers his shoulders when you touch them requires no further comment. What is causing the problem? Poor posture, bad biomechanical habits, inappropriate use of muscular force are all part of the answer, but the source of the problem is that the student is doing the move with his mind, not with his body. When we learn to let go of controlling the movements and let our bodies do the moves, based on correct understanding of how our muscle and skeleton systems work, we discover the great secret of taijiquan as an internal art: effortless power.

Letting go in push-hands includes cultivating a willingness to work with our resistance to close body contact, our fears of getting hurt, our need to win or not lose face. Letting go is supported as we acknowledge our fear, pride, laziness, aggression, lack of self-confidence and any other thing we hide from ourselves, and gently work with them until they no longer control us or remain hidden. Letting go does not mean erasing or blotting out these feelings or pushing ourselves to drop them, but making a commitment to face them in gentle awareness.

Wolfe Lowenthal, an American taiji teacher, gives a wonderful description of how we can use push-hands training as a way to study ourselves:

If in pushing I find my partner straining in resistance,
the fault also lies with my use of strength—
if I were not being so insistent he could not resist me.
Conversely, if I feel my partner's hand force
building up on my body, it is because of my resistance—
if there were no resistance, he would have nothing to push against.

— Lowenthal, 1991: 132

When we train in push-hands and let go of the need to win, the person opposite us becomes a partner, not opponent, in our joint effort to explore the true spirit of taiji: what we learn about ourselves through "investment in loss."

When teachers say that taijiquan is a life-long practice, there is often a misunderstanding at to what this means. Often students believe this refers to perfecting the different forms or mastering push-hands to the point where one always wins. But the essence of taiji has nothing to do with perfecting technique or mastering something. It has nothing to do with mastering oneself, if by that we mean controlling our thoughts and feelings or reflecting a perfect image of the Master. It is the practice of learning how to learn or resting in beginner's mind, moment to moment. It is the practice of the student who, frustrated and angry at not getting "it," starts to walk out the door, returns to his training place and makes the gentle vow, "I'll try once more."

References

Chodron, P. (1991). *The wisdom of no escape: And the path of loving kindness.* Boston: Shambhala.

Goldstein, J. (1976). *The experience of insight: A simple and direct guide to Buddhist meditation.* Boston: Shambhala.

Lowenthal, W. *There are no secrets: Professor Cheng Man-ch'ing and his tai chi chuan.* Berkeley: North Atlantic.

Suzuki, S. (1970). *Zen mind, beginner's mind.* New York: Weatherhill.

4

Thoughts on the Classic of Taijiquan
by Carol M. Derrickson, M.A.

"Using the interchange of yin-yang duality to control one's opponent."

Punch, pull, or push, Mr. Chen Xiqi remains unmovable after many varied attempts were made to topple him. The Chen-taiji stylist lives in Hangzhou, China. Photo by M. DeMarco.

Introduction

Over the years that I have been a student of taijiquan, my teachers have spoken to me of the wisdom of the taiji classics and I have read a few translations and commentaries of these classics. Somehow, the ideas never quite settled inside me, never quite made sense. Since I know some Chinese, I decided to tackle translating Wang Zongyue's *Classic of Taijiquan* myself. It's written in literary Chinese, a style quite unlike modern spoken Chinese, so the process has been a long and interesting journey toward understanding the wisdom of the classic.

The *Classic of Taijiquan* posits the essentials for completely understanding the workings of the universe as expressed in movement in martial arts. Three aspects dominate the classic as it constructs this framework: 1) defining the meaning and importance of taiji, 2) coordinating all movement in terms of the *shisan shi* or thirteen stances, and 3) using the interchange of yin-yang duality to control one's opponent. Wang argues that these essentials place the practitioner in a superior position which not only allows one to defeat opponents but offers him spiritual growth. Though a number of significant secondary themes are also woven into the text, these three repeatedly dominate the work.

My Chinese language source was a version edited by Tang Hao of Taiwan. Using the traditional literary Chinese format of adding one's own commentary to an original document, Tang incorporates his editorial comments with the *Classic of Taijiquan* by Wang Zongyue in the volume entitled *Wang Zongyue Taijiquan Ling Yanjiu*. In this study, the classic includes seven parts: 1) *Shisan Shi Lun* or "A Discussion of the Thirteen Stances," 2) *Taijiquan Lun* or "A Discussion of Taijiquan," 3) *Taijiquan Lie* or "An Explanation of Taijiquan," 4) *Shisan Shi Ge* or "Song of the Thirteen Stances," 5) *Dashou Ge* or "Song of Push-hands," 6) *Shisan Shi Xing Gong Xin Lie* or "Expounding on the Central Focus in Performing the Thirteen Stances," and 7) *Shisan Shi Mingmu* or "The Names of the Thirteen Stances."

Tang discusses historical documentation and argues that Wang Zongyue is the author; nonetheless, Wang's authorship is not verified. If Wang were indeed the author, information about him is surprisingly sketchy and inconsistent. A number of specialists place him in the Ming Dynasty (1368-1644). The piece is written in the literary Chinese of that period, which indicates that an educated person wrote the text. So, if Wang is the author, he would probably have been a member of the educated elite of traditional times. The debate over authenticity and historical documentation continues. Regardless of historical documentation, what is clear is that the ideas of the classic are sufficiently valuable that they have been handed down to succeeding generations. They are the focus of this chapter.

A number of quite competent taiji specialists have translated Wang's piece, but the quality of those translations varies considerably. For example, the opening line of Section Two, "A Discussion of Taijiquan" or *Taijiquan Lun*, is translated by Jou Tsung Hwa as follows: "Tai-Chi is born of Wu-Chi. It is the origin of dynamic and static states and the mother of Yin and Yang" (1980: 181). The same line is found in Sophia Delza's *Body and Mind in Harmony* with translation credits given to three other people: "T'ai Chi is infinity, the absolute; it is the mother of Yin and Yang, of everything male and female" (1961: 183). Whereas both translations are basically "correct," Jou's is more readable and direct.

Similar variations can be seen in translations of the next line. T. T. Liang's version in his *T'ai Chi Ch'uan for Health and Self-Defense* reads: "In motion they separate; in tranquillity they fuse into one" (1974: 33). In contrast, the same line from Lo's *The Essence of T'ai Chi Ch'uan: The Literary Tradition* reads: "It is not excessive or deficient; accordingly when it bends, it then straightens" (1979: 31). Liang's translation flows more smoothly and conveys the essence of the idea more clearly.

Part of the problem in understanding the meaning of this classic is in understanding the individual terms with their various spellings, implications, and uses. A background of Chinese philosophy is essential.

The Meaning of Taiji

Clearly identifying and differentiating the two terms *wuji* and *taiji* is the first hurdle. The two major romanization or spelling systems converting Chinese characters into Westernized spellings are Wade-Giles and Pinyin. The WadeGiles traditional spelling of the two terms are *wu chi* and *t'ai chi*. However, *t'ai chi* is often written incorrectly as *tai chi*. The Pinyin spellings, *wuji* and *taiji*, are closest to their correct pronunciation and will be used here. (When two different spellings for the same word are given hereafter, the first will be Pinyin and the second Wade-Giles, e.g., *qi/ch'i*).

In the term *wuji*, *wu* means "without" or "void"; *ji* is "to the utmost point" or "ultimate." Together they mean "ultimate void" or "ultimate nothingness." In traditional Daoist/Taoist philosophy, wuji is the creative void from which all conscious thought and all ideas spring. *Wuji* gives rise to *yi*, "intention" or "ideas."

So, *yi* means "idea," "intention," or "will," and it is the product of *wuji*. Wang asserts: "Common to everything is *yi* or intention, which does not reside in the outer aspects of movement" (Section One: 2). When the creative forces of *wuji* produce an idea, that intention is put into practice externally as *taiji*, the interplay of yin and yang.

Tai means "very," "much," "excessive," "too." Combined with *ji* as above, taiji means "very ultimate" which doesn't sound quite right in English. So, it may be translated as the "grand ultimate." Daoist philosophy conceives of *taiji* as the workings of yin and yang, the spiraling, ever-changing movement which is the physical, real-life expression of meaning or thought. From the unity of *wuji* comes the duality of *taiji*.

The duality called *yin* and *yang* is the balance of opposites which characterize the cosmos. The opposites are not in struggle against each other. For one to be healthy, happy, and effective as a martial artist, yin and yang must be in balance in every way. Yang is direct light, the sun. It is

47

hot, aggressive, dominant, the male principle, and it is also expressed in odd numbers, spicy food, cooked food, the governing vessel of the body. In contrast, yin is reflected light, the moon. It is cold, passive, yielding, the female principle, and is also expressed as even numbers, bland food, raw food, the conception vessel of the body. So, taiji is expressed as yin and yang in harmony.

Keeping these concepts clearly in mind, then, I translate the passage referred to above from the original Chinese manuscript as follows:

Taiji zhu	That which is taiji
wuji er sheng	is born from wuji
yin yang zhi mu yeo	and is the mother of yin and yang.
Dong shi ze fen,	When moving it separates,
jing zhi ze he	and when quiet it rejoins
wuguo buji	without excess or deficiency....
	– Section Two: 3

However, more important than individual words and translations are the concepts, the heart of the matter.

This passage means that each person's mind is like *wuji*, the grand void, the ultimate nothingness. It is the creative pool from which ideas, thought, and plans of action spring. It is quiet until the idea is brought into being, until action begins. And it returns to quiet when action is completed.

When movement is initiated and the plan is put into effect, taiji begins. Taiji is movement which expresses the ultimate duality, yin and yang. This interplay of opposites encompasses all movement in taijiquan. For example, in stepping one distinguishes the weighted or yang leg from the less-weighted or yin leg. Wardoff is counter-balanced by rollback, and so on.

Simply put, this principle means that in taijiquan one moves when there is a specific reason to do so. The reason may be to respond to an attack or to take advantage of an opponent's vulnerability. Whatever the reason, one moves because an intention or action plan exists which requires movement to execute it successfully.

The *Shisan Shi* or Thirteen Stances

The thirteen stances hold the key to understanding how to move properly and effectively, so Wang devotes much of the classic to discussing the meaning and importance of these movements. Specifically, the content of Sections Two, Six, and Seven focuses on these stances. Wang explains that

48

the thirteen are the combination of movements based on the traditional Five Elements or *wuxing/wu hsing* and the Eight Trigrams or *bagua/pa kua*. The thirteen stances literally form the framework of movement within which taiji is expressed by directing movement to the four major directions, the four oblique corners, and the center. By understanding the subtleties and nuances of the thirteen stances, one learns how to use them to execute any plan of action effectively.

The term translated as "stance" is *shi/shih*. It could also be expressed as "gestures" or "positions of power." *Mathews' Chinese-English Dictionary* also gives the following definitions for *shi*: power, influence, authority, strength, aspect, conditions, and circumstances (1963, #5799: 412). Though the diversity of meanings seems bewildering at first, together they have as a common theme the focus on outer appearance in a position of power or authority. By combining movement based on the Five Elements and the Eight Trigrams, Wang was indicating that such movement was a microcosm, an expression of the entire cosmic order on a small, personal scale. Moreover, the corresponding movement is inherently powerful and the stances are positions of strength. From this perspective, it is essential to understand the inherent quality of striking energy and the degree of yin-yang quality that exists in each of the stances. Wang, therefore, delineates each in detail in his text. My diagram of "The Thirteen Stances" (see page 52) visually expresses this combination of the Five Elements and the Eight Trigrams and locates the self in the cosmic order.

In traditional Chinese thought, the Five Elements were metal (literally, gold), wood, water, fire, and earth. They correspond with many aspects of health and the body. For example, they are linked with the five internal organs (lungs, liver, kidneys, heart, and spleen), and the five sense organs (nose, eyes, ears, tongue, and lips).

From the point of view of movement, each element also has a corresponding position on the compass, a quality of energy, and type of action. Metal is in the southerly position where the sun is strongest and is, therefore, a strong yang stance. Its energy type is *pi* which means "to split," "chop," "cleave," or "divide." Hence, one can *pi shou* or thrust forth the hand as in a chop. And in overall body movement, metal corresponds to the aggressive, active movement of stepping forward or advancing.

In contrast, the wood element is in the most northerly position which is colder and thoroughly yin in quality. Its energy type is *beng*, which means "to burst," "break open," or "be hit by something." So *beng lie*, for example, would be to break open by a general fist strike or a vibrating palm. In general movement, wood expresses its yin quality by yielding, retreating, or stepping backward. Just as trees or plants are passively yin, so is this type of movement.

The water element is associated with the westerly direction and works with *zuan* energy, which means "to drill, " "bore," "get into," "go through," "penetrate," "pierce." For example, *zuan xin tou gu* would be to penetrate the heart and pierce the bone using a strike which shocks one's opponent's entire physical system. Generally, the water element is linked with the act of looking to the left or regarding movement on one's left, since as one faces the north, west is on the left.

In contrast, in the easterly position is the fire element. Its energy type is *pao* which means "to fire" as a cannon; or "to put to fire," as "to fry or roast in a pan." *Pao hong* action is bombardment, pummeling one's opponent. Since east is to the right when facing north, the direction marking the rise of the fiery sun, the fire element corresponds to gazing to the right or regarding movement on the right.

The fifth element is earth which lies at the center. It corresponds to *heng*, a mixture of unrestrained violence with obstructive movement sideways or across a path. *Heng zhu le* is "to block," "to stop," "to parry." The earth element's generalized stance is to be solidly in place in a stable equilibrium. In taijiquan forms this is the stance known as *wuji* or "preparation"; the preparation move sets the stage for the plan of action which is the taijiquan form itself.

Coordinated with the Five Elements are the Eight Trigrams or *bagua/pa kua*. They are best known in the *Yijing/IChing*, which explains their relationship to the cosmos and the meaning of life. Expressed in groups of three lines, the yang lines are solid and the yin lines have one break in the center. The *bagua* are drawn as yang lines, yin lines, or varying combinations of lines. Identified by their position on the compass, each trigram expresses a type of movement, a characteristic aspect or quality, and an image. Together they guide the practitioner in perceiving the order of the cosmos.

South is expressed by the three solid lines which are completely yang, the source of the sun and heat. Its aspect is creative and dynamic; its image is Heaven or moving upward to the heavens. So in movement, the southerly trigram is aggressive as *peng* or "wardoff," a forward and upward movement.

Southwest incorporates yin as its third line; its aspect is gentle or penetrating and its image is the wind. In China, the equatorial winds move from southwest to northeast, so southwest would seem to be the source of the wind. Its movement is *cai*, meaning "to pick" or "to gather," also "to pluck" or "to pull." Wind pulls most strongly over land as a tornado, although it will also often act through simple wind gusts. Though not fully yang, its movement is still powerful. Interestingly, in contemporary Chinese, "to catch a cold" is *shangfeng*, or literally "harmed by the wind." The power attributed to wind has ancient origins.

West is two lines of yin on either side of a yang line; that creates the rudimentary form of the character meaning "water" and water is the image attributed to the west. Its aspect is abysmal. Gradually becoming more yin in quality as one approachs the north, this trigram's movement is *ji* meaning "to push against someone" or "to press." Similarly, as water presses forward it can wear away whatever lies in its path.

The trigram in the northwesterly position is a yang line over two yin lines. Its aspect is that of keeping still or being hard, and its image is that of mountains. Its hardness is yang, but its immobility is yin. The movement for northwest is *kao* or "shoulder stroke," take literally as "leaning against someone." So, in performing the shoulder stroke, one feels solid like the Himalayas, the Kunlun Mountains, or the other mountains which lie to the west-northwest of China.

North's trigram, in counterbalance to the south, is completely yin in nature and is portrayed as three broken lines. Its aspect is receptive, yielding; its image is the earth. Movement is manifested in *lu* which is "to yield" or "to rollback." Just as the earth is receptive and yields to forces acting upon it, in movement one gives way and draws energy toward oneself.

The trigram in the northeast is two yin lines above a yang. Its image is arousing and its image is thunder. As for movement, *lie* is "to split" or "split energy." With thunderstorms comes lightning, which has an arousing effect on people. Lightning also splits apart trees and other objects. So, in movement one has vibrancy and force to rend asunder.

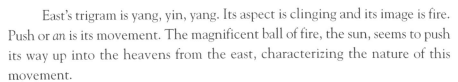

East's trigram is yang, yin, yang. Its aspect is clinging and its image is fire. Push or *an* is its movement. The magnificent ball of fire, the sun, seems to push its way up into the heavens from the east, characterizing the nature of this movement.

Southeast is a yin line over two yang lines, creating the aspect of joyousness and having the image of a lake. In movement, it is *chou* or "elbow stroke." In southeast China is a large lake region, including the famous West Lake outside of Hangzhou. One might think of nudging a friend with one's elbow to get his attention in order to share some happy event or to share the beauty of the lake.

The Thirteen Stances, Five Elements and Eight Trigrams

Trigram's Aspect =s hown in ( ). Element's Action = shown in [ ].

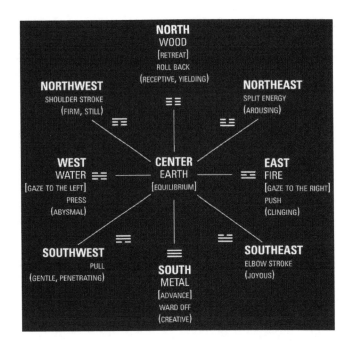

By understanding the subtleties and nuances of these thirteen stances, one can adjust one's own movement to control one's opponent. They are the key to understanding one's own yielding and aggressive energies as a miniature of the cosmic order, a reflection of the yin-yang balance of life itself. Wang remarks in the *Song of the Thirteen Stances*: "The thirteen postures as a whole should not be treated lightly. Their significance springs from the waist. They alter and revolve emptiness and solidity in accordance with the intention one has kept in mind..." (Section Four: 8). In movement properly based in the thirteen stances, then, the duality of taiji is clearly expressed. Correctly executing this duality marks the secret of success for taijiquan.

Balancing Yin and Yang Energy

With the thirteen stances, one starts at the center, forming the pivotal focus of one's own microcosm, aware of what is to the left and right and ready to advance or retreat. But as movement is initiated and one plans to move into one of the stances, an interplay of yin and yang also begins.

The classic strongly emphasizes the significance of maintaining a proper balance between the two energies, balancing the dualities in movement:

> Where there is up, there is also down; where there is left, there is also right. If one intends to move upward, then one also entertains a downward intention. If one intends to raise something upward, one must in addition employ the idea of pushing it downward. In this way its roots are naturally severed. This way invites [its] ruin, without a doubt.
>
> – Section One: 2

Though duality itself is important, how one uses the interchange effectively is what achieves success. In the same section Wang explains:

> [The concept of] emptiness and solidity ought to be clearly distinguished. Anyone place naturally has its own inherent emptiness and solidity, but each place is always in this way also unifying emptiness and solidity. The body is section by section threaded together, so not even an interval the size of a silk fiber or plant thread should be severed.
>
> – Section One: 2

Defeat is assured if the continuity is severed and an imbalance is created. Further, success is achieved and defeat is averted when the ability to yield is the focus of movement:

> By facing forward and yielding backward, one attains a strong position
> that is like the moving force of the universe. If there are areas which
> do not have such a strong stance, it is because the body is uncoordi-
> nated and movement is confused. That defect of necessity lies in the
> failure of the waist and legs. Movements upward, downward, forward,
> backward, to the left, and to the right are all like this.
>
> – Section One: 1

And even more specifically:

> If one's left is subjected to weight [from one's opponent], then the left
> should be emptied. If the right is subjected to weight, the right should
> be emptied. If [one's opponent] bends downward, then one becomes com-
> pletely unfathomable.... If the other person is moving with haste, then
> respond hurriedly. If the other person is moving slowly, follow slowly.
> Although transformed in a myriad of ways, the principle is to be as one
> string of cash (i.e. to have continuity).... The other person won't know
> me; I alone will know the other person.
>
> – Section Two: 4

Such movement is also identified by certain terms:

> When the other person is hard and unyielding and I am gentle and
> yielding is called *zou* or "withdrawing." When I move in accordance with
> another is called *zhan* or "attaching."
>
> – Section Two: 3

Ultimately, defeating the opponent comes as the result of proper
movement incorporating the acts of yielding and attaching.

Spiritual Energy as the Unifying Entity

What has been described so far is like a three-dimensional puzzle or
frame. The parts all fit together in a particular way with the self at the center
of the microcosm, and movement is in a constantly changing balance of yin
and yang based on the thirteen stances. When the opponent challenges that
microcosm, yielding and attaching are the primary means for bringing that

person under control.

The last dimension to add to the framework is the spiritual or inner aspect. Clearly identifying the terms used in the classic helps. Wang distinguishes between *qi* or "life energy" and *jing*, which is "stimulated qi" or "moving qi." These two terms are primarily dealing with the unseen but physical aspect of life force, as the classic explains:

> As one becomes experienced, one gradually apprehends and understands *jing* or "moving energy." From understanding *jing*, moreover, one by steps reaches spiritual elucidation. In this way one does not use force. Otherwise how could clear understanding be possible? ... One must understand yin and yang. Attaching, then, is yielding, and yielding is attaching. Yin is not separated form yang, and yang is not separated from yin. Yin and yang assist each other. In this way one understands how to move energy.
>
> – Section Two: 4-5

So, on the external side, yielding and not using force are essential. Internally, understanding how to move one's own energy and then moving one's opponent's energy is crucial.

Now this concept of "reaching spiritual elucidation" mentioned above is somewhat vague. The term used here is *shen*, often translated simply as "spirit." I understand the term to incorporate both the physical dimension of what T.T. Liang calls "spirit of vitality" and the internal realm which has to do with the heart and life essence. So the classic states (Section One: 1): "When the qi is properly excited, spiritual energy [*shen*] is properly practiced within." Jou cites the same idea as the Daoist principle "*lian qi hua shen*," or "transferring physical force into spiritual power" (1980: 213); in other words, through the practice of using the qi, one is transformed spirituality.

One aspect of this process resides in the concept of heart-mind, the term or concept of *xin*. In summary, the classic argues that using *xin* or heart-mind to move the qi makes the qi penetrate the bones. Using qi to move the body, therefore, is deriving benefit from the heart-mind. A light spiritual essence is thus cultivated.

From the martial arts point of view, understanding these concepts and incorporating them into one's fighting technique make one unbeatable. Or as the classic says (Section Two: 4): "A brave hero for whom there is no match is the one who cultivates this in every respect and achieves it." The classic goes even further in its claims that yielding and attaching make one's fighting successful:

> Thus, though there are a wide variety of able martial arts groups, their power and energy differ from that of taijiquan. For the most part, it doesn't go beyond the strong taking advantage of the weak, the slow yielding to the fast, those who are powerful striking the powerless, and the slow of hand yielding to the fast of hand... Note that four ounces can move aside 1000 pounds [by yielding]. It is evident that one is superior by NOT using force. Behold the form by which a seventy—or eigthty-year-old person is able to withstand a multitude. How can the fighters who focus on being fast be able to put the principles of yielding and not using force into practice?
>
> — Section Two: 4-5

This approach is one reason why taijiquan is called the "grand ultimate hand-to-hand combat."

A master exhibiting the harmonizing of yin and yang within the movements of the set. Here, in "white stork spreads wings," one leg is light while the other is weighted; One hand moving high right, while the other is weighted and low left.

My journey toward understanding the wisdom of the classic, then, goes beyond simply translating terms, creating diagrams, and defining concepts. If these are in fact the fundamental truths of the universe, what is written here goes beyond mere dictums for defeating an opponent. The classic discloses the way that we can be most stable, productive, healthy, and whole in both the physical and spiritual realms.

The problems of living and moving as a microcosm of life itself are obvious, but not insurmountable. The classic provides many examples, images, and instructions to help its readers understand and execute these important ideas. The following are paramount:

1) Let the creative void of *wuji* give rise to an intention which can be put into practice as taiji;
2) in carrying out the plan, consider the nuances of the thirteen stances and the framework of the Five Elements and the Eight Trigrams in choosing the one(s) which match the problem; and
3) incorporate the harmony of yin and yang as they interplay in yielding and attaching to one's opponent.

These suggestions should not only bring victory but also spiritual understanding, creating a wholeness or melding of the physical, spiritual, and cosmic realms.

References

Cao, Zhiqing. (1988). *Xingyiquan lilun yanjiu.* Beijing: Renmin Tiyu Publications.

Delza, Sophia. (1961). *Body and mind in harmony: T'ai chi ch'uan.* New York: Cornerstone Library.

Jou, Tsung Hwa. (1980). *The tao of tai-chi chuan.* Piscataway, NJ: Tai Chi Foundation.

Liang, T. T. (1974). *T'ai chi ch'uan for health and self-defense.* New York: Random House.

Lo, Benjamin Pang Jeng. (1979). *The essence of t'ai chi chuan: The literary tradition.* Berkeley, CA: North Atlantic Books.

Mark, Bow-Sim. (1979). *Taijiquan genben jiaocai.* Taiwan: Shijian Press.

Mathews, R. H. (1963). *Mathews' Chinese-English dictionary.* Cambridge, MA: Harvard University Press.

Tang, Hao, ed. (1971). *Wang Zongyue taijiquan jing yanjiu.* Taiwan: Haulin Publishers.

Wu, Jinrong, Ed. (1983). *The pinyin Chinese-English dictionary.* Beijing: The Commercial Press.

5

The Necessity for Softness in Taijiquan
by Michael A. DeMarco, M.A.

Snake Creeps Downward. Illustration by Mary E. Tanner.

In the whole world, nothing is softer and weaker than water.
And yet for attacking the hard and strong, nothing can beat it
Because there is nothing you can use to replace it.
That water can defeat the unyielding —
That the weak can defeat the strong —
There is no one in the whole world who doesn't know it,
And yet there is no one who can put it into practice.
— Ch. 78, *Lao-Tzu Te-Tao Ching**

*Henricks, R. (Trans.). (1989). *Lao-tzu te-tao ching.* New York: Ballantine Books.

For Daoists, water has long been the ultimate symbol for illustrating proper actions. Its unique characteristics offer insights into the Way (*Dao*) of movement which, when applied to the martial arts, gives lessons on how to improve our practice and execution of technique. Through the practice of the various styles of taijiquan that are executed in a relaxed, slow and easy manner, the practitioner can feel the subtleties that allow one's movement to become like water, moving in harmony with the Way.

What is so unique about the nature of water that can be usefully applied in martial arts practice? Water is soft and yielding. However, a river, in travelling thousands of miles from its source to the ocean, must overcome countless rigid obstacles. In the martial arts, someone defending himself must overcome whatever obstacles his opponent may present, be they physical or psychological attacks. Like water with its ability to change form, a person can best defend himself from attack by yielding. Throw a rock into a pond and the water allows the rock to take its course. It yields to the rock while encompassing it. Throw a rock against a tree and see the damage done.

For defense against any aggressive movement, yielding proves to be very effective. A target cannot be hit if it is not present. In the practice of taijiquan, one quickly learns to yield to an incoming attack. In like manner, one learns to flow with the opposite forces which may draw one onward, such as being pulled forwards. When attacks are neutralized in this fashion, it also becomes possible to eliminate any further threat from the attacker by an appropriate technique, i.e., joint lock, throw, or strike. Although relaxed, the response can be executed quite powerfully, much like the concerted force exhibited by a typhoon. Even air, which is often described as "nothing," becomes increasingly dangerous as it transforms from breeze, to wind, to hurricane, to tornado.

In this chapter, we present a few exercises designed to train the martial art practitioner to move more naturally. The following exercises focus on the necessity of softness in order to find the inter-relatedness of unified body movement, the flowing ease of proper technique, and the balance necessary for stability. Above all, these exercises should bring about a "feel" for natural movement that can be applied to the range of self-defense techniques. Some applications from the Yang taijiquan form will then be presented to show how these theories can be applied to any technique.

Exercises: The Way of Taijiquan Body Movement

In addition to softness and yielding, water also illustrates other important characteristics worthy of observation. Because of gravity, water seeks equilibrium as shown in the level surface of a pond. It sinks to the lowest level while remaining even at the surface, much like the well-balanced postures of taijiquan. Water flows and shifts. Since taijiquan is based on the principles of yin and yang, each taiji form flows smoothly one into another. A river moves as one and the techniques strung together to form the taiji set likewise move as one continuous stream. The following exercise will illustrate some of the natural, water-like qualities necessary for doing taijiquan properly.

Exercise One: Taking the First Step

Take a single step. This is something we do every day of our lives, but seldom do we take the time to notice just what the movement entails. Take a single step and ask yourself, "How did I do it?" There are two basic ways to step forward. One is to quickly lift up one leg, lean to the front to place the foot down, and fall forward onto the extended foot. The second way follows the taijiquan principles and is shown in the following photos. The complete process for taking a step should be done in a balanced and relaxed manner.

1-A   The body is erect and balanced with weight distributed equally on both feet. This position is natural and relaxed.

1-B   Slowly shift the body weight totally onto the right leg while keeping the spine straight. This allows the body to remain in balance and frees the left leg for making the step forward. If you did not shift the weight while lifting the foot, you'd fall!

1-C If the right leg remains stiff, the left leg could be placed to the front by the body falling forward. Rather than do this, keep the body erect and sink by bending the right knee.

1-D The sinking movement allows the left heel to be placed forward. The distance of the step depends on how much one sinks. The weight remains on the back leg until the left heel touches the floor.

1-E Slowly shift the weight forward. The toes of the left foot will gradually rest on the floor as the shift occurs. The left knee bends as the back leg straightens. The weight is about 70% on the front foot.

Exercise Two: Letting the Arms Fall Up

Have you seen movies in which a person slips on a banana peel? He loses his footing, as if he had a rug pulled out from under him. As he loses his footing, his hands fly into the air. Some taijiquan movements also illustrate this natural reaction.

2-A, 2-B, and 2-C Begin as in 1-A, only with the arms hanging freely. Then let your knees buckle and fall freely into a squat. If the arms are relaxed, they will effortlessly move upwards. The movement must be done rather quickly to have this effect on the arms. Just as yin complements yang, the sinking motion is complemented by the rising motion of the arms. If you do this movement in slow motion, it becomes necessary to consciously raise the arms. However, the movement will seem easier and the arms lighter when done after this practice than if one relies solely on muscle power to raise the arms. The movement will seem like the arm movement of a water pump. As one end moves downward (the body), the other moves upward (the arms).

Exercise Three: Interconnected Arm Movement

Open a door. It can open only as far as its hinges allow. The following exercise allows one to feel the restrictions a tense body can place on itself. When the body moves as a whole in a relaxed manner, movements become easier and the body flows freely without straining muscles or joints.

3-A   Stand with the right arm forward.

3-B   While keeping the body rigid, move the right arm as far as possible to the right side. You will feel the right shoulder muscles bunch together and an uncomfortable pulling in the socket. This exercise allows one to feel the effects of doing the movement incorrectly.

3-C thru 3-G Start again as in 3-A. While keeping the body rigid, let the right arm fall downward by its own weight. Again, you will feel the arm abruptly stop.

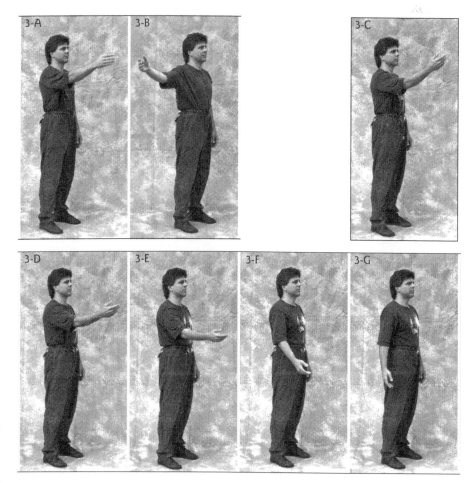

63

3-H thru 3-K. Try the preceding sequence (3-C thru 3-G) once more, but in a relaxed manner. This will allow your hips and shoulders to rotate with the falling weight of the right arm. The natural arc of the arm falling will be a direct line from front to back and the arm will naturally "fall upwards" due to its own weight and speed during the free-fall. The body will also shift to the right leg and the left heel will rise to follow in the direction of the arm movement. The head will also follow the movement as if you were looking, while pointing with the right hand, at an object behind you.

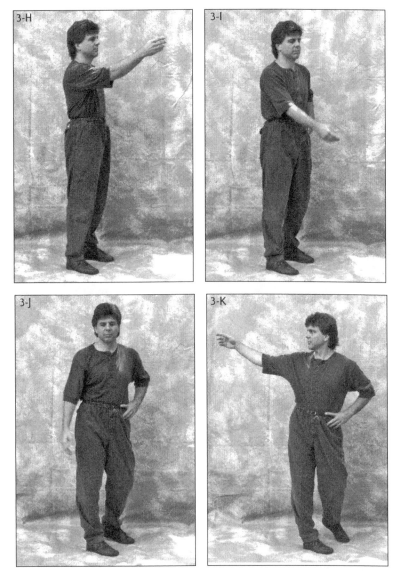

Exercise Four: Interconnected Leg Movement

This exercise has the same purpose as the previous one, except it focuses on the leg and hip movement rather than the arm and shoulder.

4-A Stand with all your weight the left leg (weighted; yang characteristic) and place the right heel out to the right side (empty; yin characteristic). Face in the direction of your right foot.

4-B Turn the head and hips ninety-degrees to the left so that you are looking in the direction of your left foot. You can alternate the movement back and forth from the original position. Did your right foot also turn in the same direction? If not, there may be too much weight on the right leg. Or perhaps the lower body is rigid. Proper shifting of weight, as the alternating between yin and yang, is a prerequisite for smooth, well-balanced movements.

Exercise Five: Rope-like Arms Led by Waist Movement

Taiji classics state that all movements start in the waist. However, many practitioners execute movements with tensed hands, arms and shoulders. This is true particularly with punches, pushes, and pulls. The body often automatically tenses at the thought of needing additional power. But taiji does not solely rely on arm muscles for power. Power is generated by the integrated body movement. The following exercise can be repeated by alternating the swing to the left and right. In addition to turning the waist on its axis, the player can augment the same movement by shifting his weight by pushing off the back leg, e.g., the left leg when turning right.

5-A thru 5-D. Begin with the stance shown in 5-A and concentrate on letting the arms hang in a relaxed manner as if they were ropes hanging from the shoulders. Turn the waist to the left and feel how the arms swing in the same direction. As the waist turns, the shoulders turn, moving the upper arms and then the forearms naturally follow. This is not a machine-like movement. The parts will follow one another, just as a whip is directed by its handle. But, as the handle is pulled back, the whip's tip is still moving forward until it strikes its target.

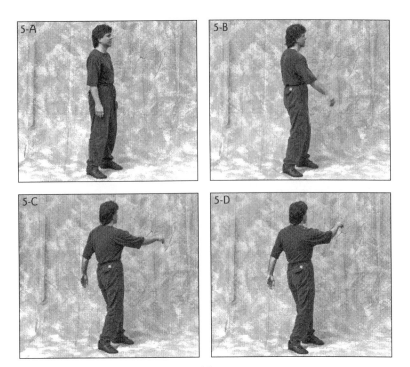

Applications

The following taiji boxing movements illustrate the necessity for softness in executing self-defense techniques. The movements embody the principles upon which taijiquan is based, such as relaxation, balance, fluid change, and integrated body movement. Study the photos and practice the techniques to feel these principles in movement.

While utilizing these principles can greatly improve martial skills, they also are conducive to physical and mental fitness. When smoothness is attained in executing these techniques, the joints and muscles will not be overexerted or overextended, eliminating the threat of injuring ourself through improper practice. The skeletal system will be in proper alignment with the movements. First practice both the exercises and applications in slow motion. Gradually increase the speed of the techniques but be sure to apply the taiji principles! As an end result, the movements should feel powerful, yet relaxed.

Application One: Wardoff

Wardoff is a basic but important movement and, therefore, often repeated in the taiji set. The application here shows a technique which can follow a previous block by the right forearm for an incoming right-hand punch. Note that balance is maintained throughout and the left arm follows the rotation of the waist as the weight is shifted from the right leg to the left. It is not necessary to be tense. Since the attacker's strike was deflected, he chooses to withdraw. The defender simply "goes with the flow" to thwart the attacker from regaining his balance and topples the attacker by accelerating him in the direction of his retreat. Compare this movement to Exercise One.

All photos by Pete Gool. Special thanks to Peter Danielewicz
for his help in demonstrating the techniques with the author.

67

Application Two: Rollback

In Rollback, the left hand can be used to intercept a strike and deflect it. While executing the strike with force and momentum, the attacker can easily throw himself off-balance if the strike does not reach its target. The defender, therefore, moves in the same general direction as the incoming force, easily guiding the strike downward and thus drawing the attacker further off-balance to the ground. Note how the defender has shifted his weight from the front to the back foot as in Exercise Three. The hand placed on the attacker's left elbow is an added precaution.

Application Three: Jade Lady Works at Shuttle

One of the applications for Jade Lady can be seen when an attacker grabs the raised arm of a person with the intent to strike him. Since the arm was raised, he tries to strike at the mid-section. Although grabbed firmly, the defender keeps his right arm relaxed and moves with the slight pull from the attacker. As the attacker steps in to deliver a left punch, the defender turns his waist to the right causing the strike to glance off and also be blocked by the left arm. The left arm literally falls into its defensive position by flowing with the body's turn. The attacker, now off-balance, realizes his critical position and starts to retreat. The defender keeps contact by keeping his left arm against the attacker's right arm. Moving with the attacker's retreat, the defender controls the rest of the movement and adds a right hand push to drive the attacker away. The push could be changed to a strike if so desired. A variety of principles can be found in Jade Lady as shown in the exercises given on the previous pages.

Application Four: Monkey Retreats

By its very name, Monkey Retreats illustrates a backward movement, which follows the same taiji principles discussed earlier. Some actions in the sequence are the reverse of those executed during a forward movement. For example, rather than step with the heel first, the toe is placed on the ground. The block/deflect is still made in the direction of the attacker's strike and the necessary sinking, shifting and turning remain the same as in forward movements.

The attacker and defender are near each other. As the attacker swings his left fist around at the side of the defender's head, the defender begins his defensive movement. His body shifts and sinks to his left leg, allowing the right leg to be free to step backwards. As this occurs, the right hand "falls upward" due to the momentum and is in position to deflect the attack safely to the side. The defender simultaneously places his left hand on the attacker's chest to check his movement. The left hand could be used to strike the attacker if so desired. Note that the defender's left foot is now empty of weight, and the body's turning pulls the foot into alignment with the hips. If the left leg is tensed or if too much weight remains on it, the toes would remain planted pointing straight forward or even to the left and outside the direction the hips are pointing.

It is hoped that by practicing the exercises and applications presented above, one can come to observe more closely the taiji principles discussed and their importance and usefulness for taijiquan as an art form, a system of self-defense, a moving meditation, and a holistic health system.

6

Inner Circle Taiji Training Exercises
by Stuart Kohler, M.A.

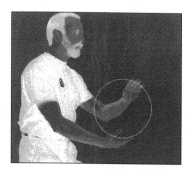

Photographs courtesy of Jim Eaton.

The *taiji* classics offer insights into the art for taiji players of all levels: and can also help resolve common frustrations for the practitioner. Students, particularly new students in the West, often feel they must invest years of training time and effort before they will master a form which yields the return they seek. One response is for teachers to offer a "short" form, while another is to offer training in which feeling is emphasized over precision of form. Some traditional training styles focus more on exactness of individual postures, which will later be linked into a single, flowing whole.

A study of the taiji classics suggests a method by which accuracy of postures need not be sacrificed for feeling in order to attain experiential understanding of continuous energy flow. This insight is derived from the delight of the "effortless effort" to be found in the practice of taijiquan, which cultivates the circulation of energy which, in turn, promotes health and, for the martial artist, power. I call this approach "Inner Circle Training."

The following quote from Song Chijian's "Twelve Guiding Principles," based on his *T'ai Chi Ch'uan Hsueh* [*Taijiquan Xue*], points to an essential circularity in the movements comprising the routine:

> The movements of [taijiquan] all advance in a circular line. When the
> forward and backward movements of [taijiquan] are connected, large or
> small circles are formed. If one's movements can be rounded out, then
> they will be lively and agile. If the body moves like a cartwheel and the

hands follow the body movements, then the movements will naturally be circular. In this way the forms turning left and right, rounded and lively, will be like shooting stars.

– Gallagher, 1989: 29

Simply stated, the premise of "Inner Circle Taiji Training" is that all postures are circular in nature, even those which may first appear to be strictly linear. By encouraging "play" to find the circles and deliberately exaggerating those circles, students are often able to experience a flow of energy much earlier in their taiji careers than would otherwise be possible.

One additional comment about inner circles also applies to all of the external or observable circles throughout the form. While circles are composed of inward and outward energy, a true circle is not composed of two pieces which are joined together (no matter how smoothly). Inbound energy is often gathering or coiling energy, as in Press or Push, in other words, a loading of the spring which will be released as part of the same single, fluid motion on the outbound phase. (The reverse may also be true, as in a posture such as Needle at Sea Bottom [nai di zen]. The extension may be seen as the "loading" energy, while compression is the releasing energy. The intention here is to stress continuous fluid movement over linear sequences, no matter how seamlessly connected.)

Before examining postures taken from the taiji routine, we must first consider the gesture of a simple circle made by the hand. Notice that a fluid circle made by the hand is actually articulated by the wrist and elbow, and, to a lesser extent, the shoulder and waist (the involvement of the lower joints will be noted later). As the circle is made smaller and more subtle, it may be observed that the smallest and most subtle hand-circle is principally formed by the wrist. As one continues to refine the size and subtlety, external (observable) movement ceases, but there remains the sensation or intent of circular movement. This is the experience of the "inner circle."

As a first example from the routine, consider the postures wardoff and rollback and, in particular, the transition between them (this and all following examples are taken from Yang style taiji). From the rounded peng energy of wardoff, the right hand extends out, fingers rotate up and the hand spirals inward as rollback is formed. There are actually several places in this sequence where continuous energy flow may be interrupted. Any interruption establishes a "dead spot" in which energy has been exhausted and has not yet been renewed. Yang Chengfu in his Ten Essential Points of Taijiquan states:

When the old strength has been exhausted and the new is not yet developed, one can very easily be controlled by an opponent. ... From beginning to end it [mind-intent rather than muscular force] continues fluidly without interruption; completing a cycle and beginning again, it flows in an endless circle and is never exhausted.

– Gallagher, 1989: 22

Such an interruption may occur if the right hand extends outward, stops at its fullest extension, then reverses direction to form the upright arm of rollback (Figures la-1c). To form what Yang Chengfu calls an "endless circle," it is helpful to imagine the lead hand as making a "flicking" movement, rolling the focus of energy from the center of the hand at wardoff out to the fingers and fingertips at the fullest extension and then allowing the energy focus to return to the palm as rollback is formed (Figures 2a-2e). Another inner circle is found in the forward hand of rollback as it circles in and up into the forward hand of press. This circle keeps the forward hand from waiting (exhausted energy) while the rear hand circles up to join and form Press.

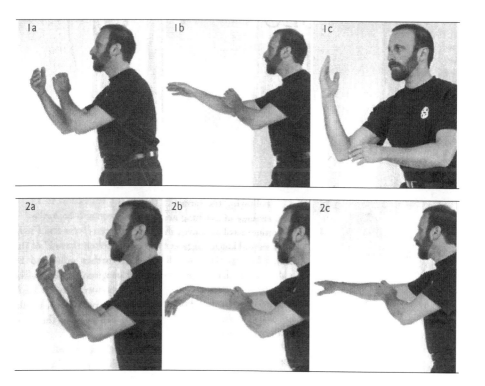

1a-b-c: Incorrect rollback sequence. 2a-b-c: Correct rollback sequence.

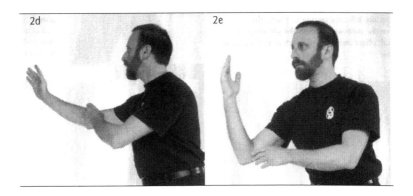

Following the formation of Press is the transition to Push. The analogy of catching and immediately passing a basketball is sometimes used to convey the transition between Press and Push. This mental image suggests fluidity, the "unbroken thread" of the taiji classics. This visualization may be further enhanced by adding a circular image. Thus, instead of imagining a piston-like in-and-out motion, which is linear (and, therefore, has a "dead" moment of transition between in and out, Figures 3a-3c), thinking of this motion in terms of a subtle circle can improve the energy flow in this transition (Figures 4a-4f).

Incorrect press-push sequence.

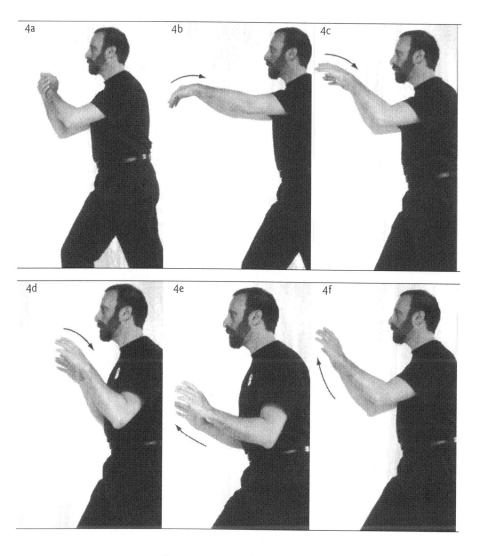

Correct press-push sequence.

In playing with the inner circle concept here as well as in all postures, one would be well advised to follow Wang Zongyue's advice in his *Mental Elucidation*: "At first let your movements be open and expanded; later make them small and compact" (Gallagher, 1989: 49). In training, gestures can be deliberately exaggerated to show the circle, later to refine and reduce the size of the gesture while still retaining the feeling found in the larger gesture. Thus, on the inbound motion of Push, the arms lift as well as retreat; on the outbound motion, the arms depress as they extend, the overall effect being a subtle vertical circle executed in front of the body.

Thrusting Hand/Palm (*chuan zhang*), found in the third section of the traditional Yang style long form, offers an inner circle in a posture usually considered inherently linear. From the completion of High Pat Horse (*gao tan ma*), the left hand must drop, however slightly, to clear the right arm. The common error here is to move the left arm as a piston which established a "dead spot" at the transition between the inbound and outbound motion (Figures 5a-5c). A circular gesture made by the left hand and arm creates an uninterrupted flow of energy which also incorporates the adjustment of height necessary to clear the right arm (Figures 6a-6f).

Incorrect thrusting hand sequence.

Correct thrusting hand sequence.

76

As a third example, let us examine the Beginning posture (*qi shi*). Traditionally, students are instructed to allow the arms to rise, wrists leading (as if balloons were tied by strings to their wrists) until the forearms are shoulder height or roughly parallel to the floor. Next the fingertips extend, making a single line from the shoulder. The common linear flaw here is that these gestures are treated as two separate movements, thereby occasioning the possibility of a "dead spot" between the point at which the arms have finished rising and before the fingertips begin their extension. To help prevent this, create the mental image of a single rounded movement, beginning with the rising arms, which is extended by moving energy out to the fingertips, again in almost a "flicking" gesture from the wrist.

Continuing with the Beginning, the elbows become heavy as the hands draw in towards the body. At the completion of this gesture, the fingertips rotate up and then the hands arc down from the elbows to complete Beginning. An inner circle may be found as the hands draw inward rather than coming to a stop at the closest point and then allowing the fingers to rotate up. The inner circle here connects the motion of the hands as they draw inward, arc back, up and around, and "flick" forward from the wrist to form a circle to the front. This is followed by the hands moving in a rounded arc downward, which traditionally completes Beginning. No matter how smoothly these movements are connected, unless the player internalizes the associated inner circles, Beginning may only aspire to be a series of smoothly connected linear pieces.

A reference to the continuous flow of inner circles may be found in the first line of the *Zhang Sanfeng Classic*: "In every movement the entire body must be light and spirited and all its parts connected like a string of pearls" (Gallagher, 1989: 47). Imagine the flow and arc of a string of pearls (even better if imagined underwater or moving in slow motion) in this same movement. In most of the examples cited in this chapter, the focus has been on the arms, hands and fingers as forming the "string of pearls." It is important to remember, however, that our brief discussion gives us only a partial view and is, therefore, only partially accurate. As found later in the *Zhang Sanfeng Classic*:

> The energy is rooted in the feet, rises through the legs, is controlled by the waist, and is formed in the fingers. From the feet to the legs to the waist, all must act as an integrated whole, so that in advancing and retreating, one can attain the proper preconditions and the position of strength.
>
> – Gallagher, 1989: 47

An example of a full-body generation of energy would be the waist circling of rollback. Energy from the rooted feet and legs sets the waist circling in motion, which in turn generates the circular movement of the arms. Specifically, from the extension of the leading arm, it is the turning of the waist which pulls that arm into its circle (Figures 7a-7b). The importance of this insight can be seen in the difference between pulling a rope with just the arms and shoulders and pulling that same rope with energy generated from the rooted feet, legs and waist-in effect, a classic form of "wind-up."

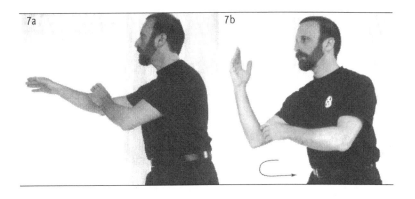

The waist in rollback sequence

Revisiting Thrusting Hand/Palm, notice that again it is the waist circling to the left which generates the inbound circling of the thrusting hand (Figures 8a-8b). If the waist remains stationary, the thrusting hand has only isolated arm and shoulder energy and power. Similarly, the outbound part of the thrusting hand circle is generated by the waist circle to the right.

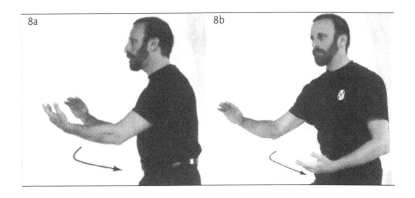

The waist in thrusting hand sequence

Again, it should be stated here that the exaggerated, "overt" circles are training exercises only; they are not meant to be taken as instruction in the correct execution of any given posture. Rather, it is a training technique intended to assist in achieving an experiential understanding of energy flow continuity in the form and the real, if subtle, sources of power in the postures. As a training technique, one should work to develop fluidity by exaggerating the circles, refining them later by reducing the external size while retaining the inner circular intent. This style of training in no way condones a form which lacks precision by encouraging one posture to be mindlessly merged into the next. In fact, when undertaken with sincerity, inner circle training will lead to a much higher level of mastery in doing the forms precisely.

Practice with the mind-intent of seeing circles in every gesture, especially those which appear to be inherently linear. The true goal of inner circle training is to internalize the circles so that they indeed become unobservable to others. All that should remain observable of inner circle training is greater smoothness, the absence of jerky start/stop linear gestures and the experience of the entire body as "light and spirited and all its parts connected like a string of pearls."

	Wade-Giles	Pinyin	Chinese
People	Chang[1] San[1]-feng[1]	Zhang[1]San[1]feng[1]	張三丰
	Yang[2] Cheng-fu[3]	Yang[2] Cheng[2]fu[3]	楊澄甫
	Wang[2] Tsung[1]-yueh[4]	Wang[2] Zong[1] yue[4]	王宗岳
Classic	T'ai[4] Chi[2] Ch'uan[2] Hsueh[2]	tai[4] ji[2]quan[2] xue[2]	太極拳學

Movements

Beginning posture	ch'i[3] shih[4]	qi[3] shi[4]	起勢
Sea Bottom Needle	hai[3] ti[3] chen[1]	hai[3] di[3] zhen[1]	海底針
Push	chi[3]	ji[3]	擠
Press	an[4]	an[4]	按
Thrusting Hand/Palm	ch'uan[1] chang[3]	chuan[1] zhang[3]	穿掌
High Pat Horse	kao[1] tan[1] ma[3]	gao[1] tan[1] ma[3]	高探馬

Reference

Gallagher, P. (1989). *Drawing silk: A manual for t'ai chi.* Guilford, VT: Deer Mountain Taoist Academy.

• 7 •

Principles and Practices in Taijiquan

by Peter Lim Tian Tek

Mr. Xia Tao (L.), President of the Hangzhou Wushu
Association, practicing tuishou with Mr. Jiang Jialun.
Photograph courtesy of Don Mainfort.

Taijiquan is both a martial art and a health art and its correct practice brings benefits in both areas. To practice correctly, a proper understanding of the theories behind the practice is required. The following is a short discussion of some of the more important theories pertaining to both health and combat.

BASIC PRINCIPLES

Loose with No Tension (*song*)

Relax and loosen all the joints so that they are flexible, connected and able to integrate properly. Proper posture is held with the minimum of muscular exertion. Gravity provides the downward stacking mechanics that establishes a power source from the feet being rooted to the ground. Proper relaxation provides more efficient use of muscles resulting in a pliable strength rather than tensed strength.

I prefer to translate *song* as "no tension" rather than "relaxation," which too often implies limpness. Why is there a need for *song?* Very simply because if you are not *song* the muscles are not able to work efficiently. Muscles tense when the antagonistic muscle groups have in some way impeded the motion of each other, as such tension is the retained energy of the movement. This results in reduced mobility, promotes fatigue and reduces power. *Jing* travels through a strike much like a wave or pulse with relaxed musculature conducting it with no retained tension. This is similar to a whip which has no tension but is able to deliver a telling strike.

Stability by Sinking (*wen, chen*)

Stability is a result of coordinating our body structure with the downward pull of gravity creating a net force against the earth from both body weight and the downward projection of mass through a single point identified as the "root." Lowering the center of gravity is essential to stability. Therefore, we should become aware of our center and thus feel the resulting stability in our movements.

Agility (*ling*)

Agility is a result of not being double-weighted or having a "dead rooting." By maintaining only one point of substantial contact with the ground you can gain the ability to move quickly, much like a ball which moves easily across the ground because it only has one point of contact with it.

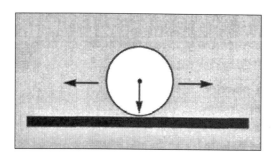

A ball has only one contact
point with the ground and so can
move freely in any direction.

The key is the word "center." We should avoid dead rooting. The idea is to lower your center of gravity to your proper focus at the dantian. There it should have a net downward force but be hung from the torso in the correct location. This would give you a centered but light feeling. If you are trying to get your center to the root of your feet, that is not centeredness. Ask yourself where the center of your body is and there is where the mass of the center should be. Some methodologies involving external and internal practices were adopted to train for this centering. The external way of training is to force the center down as far as it can go by sinking. This causes the musculature supporting the downward force to return a force from the feet back up toward the center. The internal method would first locate the center of gravity and then develop proper body posture to support it. When that is done, one should slowly lower the stance over time without sacrificing proper balance and body alignment.

Sensitivity (*ming gan*)

One of the keys in taijiquan combat is to train by focusing the mind (*yi*) on each motion. Focus the conscious mind, but also allow the subconscious to respond and become more aware. We need sensitivity to detect where our center is and where there are flaws in posture that can be exploited by an attacker. This sensitivity likewise allows us to detect an opponent's energy and movement.

Roundness (*yuan*)

The roundness of physical movement denotes a smooth connection and efficient transfer of force and energy. Hence, in the taiji postures, seek roundness. Roundness also helps in the dissipation of incoming energy.

Not Losing Contact, Not Resisting

Bu diu bu ding means literally "not losing contact, not resisting" and is perhaps one of the most descriptive terms of taiji combat. *Peng* and its characteristics is what enables this to occur. *Peng* is expansive in nature; it has the qualities of sticking and buoyancy and stability. If your opponent retreats, it follows, if he advances, it sticks and redirects.

In cultivating this principle, we need to understand that sticking is necessary in order to "listen" to your opponent's strength and understand it so you can counter it by turning it against himself. Proper "listening" makes it possible for you to detect gaps and flaws in his posture and turn them to your advantage. At the same time, the buoyant quality makes it hard for your opponent to detect your center.

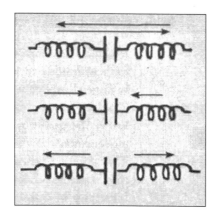

Top: Not letting go; Not resisting. Middle: Resisting. Bottom: Letting go.
Drawings of springs help illustrate the above concepts.

Breathing

Breathing initially should be natural and abdominal. As you learn how to "swim in air," the air assumes a heavy quality not unlike water. You will find that it takes relaxed effort to generate the movement. As a result of this, the breathing pattern will naturally change to your abdomen, expanding when you push out, the way it does when you are pushing a car. This is the point where reverse breathing becomes natural. It should be a natural transition and should not be forced. Practicing reverse breathing by itself to isolate the dantian and its movements in qigong should also not be forced. Reverse breathing occurs when the abdomen is pulled inward on inhaling and extend it on exhaling.

PRACTICES

Three Heights and Four Frames

The three heights are high, middle and low; the four frames are slow, fast, large, small. These denote the different ways of doing the taijiquan routine, each for a specific purpose.

The Three Heights

- **Middle:** This is the normal way we practice with the knees slightly bent and the body lowered. Here is where we learn the movements, their coordination, transition and focus.
- **Low:** At this level, our thighs should be at least parallel to the ground. One gets to this level progressively from the middle frame.

It adds to the difficulty of the form and aids in further development in regards to endurance, body connection and coordination, stability and strength.

• **High:** At this level, we refine the body connection and coordination so that the techniques can be effected with minimal movement.

The author demonstrating the rollback (top) and
push postures in three heights: high, medium, and low.
Photographs courtesy of Peter Lim Tian Tek.

The Four Frames

• **Slow:** By practicing in this manner, we learn to coordinate the taiji movements and transitions and establish the foundation that make good taiji boxing skills.

• **Large:** Practicing movements in an extra-large fashion facilitates stretching and develops resiliency, good circulation and proper muscular development. It also allows the movement comprising each technique to be savored and fully understood. It is usually done slowly as well.

- **Fast:** The techniques can also be executed quickly but without losing the qualities obtained by training slowly and with large movements.
- **Small:** This practice refines taiji techniques to their essentials so that they can be effected with minimum effort and movement. Normally in training, after learning the middle-height set and slow frame, one may commence to a fast set at a slightly lower height. However, one must retain the same qualities as before, being relaxed, sunk, and connected. Then a practitioner may move on to an even lower height at a slower speed with large movements. Lastly, one finally practices at a high height with small movements. This was the way Yang Banhou trained his students.

Form and Training

The form teaches us the content of the art, allowing us to know ourselves and how we function. Tuishou and other two-person exercises expand on this knowledge and teach us also how to know others. In knowing ourselves and knowing others we can "conquer them a hundred times out of a hundred." The form teaches us how our body can function efficiently and how it moves, what makes it live and what makes it effective. We learn here how to experience and control what we loosely refer to as "energy," "vitality principle," "vector energy," "*jing*" or "*qi*." The form is a means to experience, cultivate and learn how to effectively use this energy.

This energy is manifested through what is called "opening and closing" and has its origins in breath. This energy movement denotes the internal form (*nei xing*) and the physical movement denotes the external form (*wai xing*). In the beginning, the internal form comes from and is molded by the external form, but later the external form follows the dictates of the internal form. In the beginning, the mind directs the movements and is distinct from it. Later, the mind and the movement are one. The mind and body, internally and externally, fuse to become one entity, one reality. This is necessary for quick reactions and for the body and mind to act together to make the most of the situation.

This mind-body coordination and synthesis should become instinctive. As one becomes more dependent on the internal form and the flow of internal energy, the focus on the external form diminishes. The internal energy will be manifested through the external form. The mind and energy become the primary considerations at this level of practice. This is where the energy acts as the mind dictates; the body acts as the energy dictates. Ego and thought have no place as one moves according to the principles of the energy, to blend and balance with and to nullify the incoming flow of energy from an opponent's attack. The physical weapon is activated by the force within it although this force is an energy that is distinct from the weapon. This is internal boxing and its internal strategies for combat.

Push-hands (*tuishou*) and Sparring Hands (*sanshou*)

In taijiquan, tuishou is a practice to achieve several major goals:

1) To develop sensitivity to your opponent's motion and its origin.
2) To develop the ability to effortlessly redirect your opponent's motion by detecting and utilizing the weak vector of his motion.
3) To apply and practice a flexible rooting with fixed and moving steps while responding to your opponent's strength and motion.

Tuishou was also called *roushou* (soft hands) to emphasize non-resistance. It is not a combat practice. *Sanshou*, which is the application of the sensitivity and effortlessness developed through tuishou in a combat situation (blows, kicks, locks, grabs, etc), is the actual combative training in taijiquan. Free fighting is free form *sanshou* and is as close as you can get to combat without actually having someone out to hurt you. The Yang school has an eighty-eight posture (forty-four per person), fixed-form *sanshou*, which is akin to fixed-form sparring. The set was designed to slowly prepare the practitioner for free-form fighting or sparring. *Ting jing* (listening to *jing*) is paramount in taijiquan, since it is only by being sensitive enough to detect your opponent's motion, its qualities and its origin (this is the most important) that you can control him.

The two-person taijiquan set has specific training methodologies and goals. Fixed steps train one's sensitivity, stability and power within a limited range of motion. Moving steps expand this training to a simple back-and-forth motion by moving with self-controlled balance while avoiding being controlled by your opponent. *Dalu* (great rollback) adds the corner movements so that the repertoire is not limited to back-and-forth. Besides including the remaining four fundamental techniques, *dalu* teaches that retreat is also a form of attack. Free-form push-hands combines all the elements but still limits practice to the basic push-hands parameters. The following are goals for free-form push-hands:

1) To achieve sensitivity through contact.
2) To use that sensitivity to find the flaws in the attacker's defense. This is done by neither resisting nor letting go of an opponent's attack. The movements should be proactive in that you do not resist his motion but redirect it using its inherent flaws. In this way, the defensive movement need not only neutralize the attacking motion, but may be turned into a counterattack as well.
3) To apply the principles cultivated in the form (correct posture, rooting, sensing energy, knowledge of your own center, etc.) in a reactive situation with a partner.
4) To learn the basics of attack and defense through the use of effortless power born of proper rooting, posture and motion.

"Attracting to emptiness" simply means presenting the opponent a target which is actually a trap to lead him into emptiness (neutralizing and causing his force and momentum to act against himself). When this is done properly, your opponent's "thousand-pound force" can be deflected and used against him by the simple application of "four ounces" on the weakest vector of the incoming force to alter its trajectory back to the origin. One of the keys of taijiquan is never to use more than four ounces and never to receive more than four ounces (not exactly four ounces, mind you, the term simply indicates a light force). Accurate distancing and timing are necessary to accomplish such advanced techniques.

In Hangzhou city, Jin Huiying (R.) practices taiji applications with her student Wu Hangxin. Two-person practices help develop sensitivity necessary to improve one's form and technique. Photograph courtesy of Don Mainfort.

Is push-hands a win or lose competition? No, it isn't. It is a form of training in which both parties benefit. Oftentimes good teachers will let one party do the pushing and the other do the countering. This teaches one to detect the center and the other to avoid detection and to counter. Winning or losing should not be important at this level of training as the goal is for the partners to train each other in knowing themselves and each other.

Beating Big with Small, Fast with Slow

"Beating big with small" usually means overcoming a big force with a lesser one. This is attained by not directly opposing the big force but redirecting it to our advantage by adding a smaller force to change the trajectory of the larger force. "Beating fast with slow" means beating a faster moving opponent with a slower technique. How is this achieved? No matter how fast an attacking limb is, it is always slower than the body behind it or the last joint between it and the body. By affecting the body directly via the center, by avoiding the fast moving end and attacking the middle or last joint of the limb, we need not move as fast as we would normally need to meet the fast end of the limb and stop it. It is also easier to change its ultimate trajectory by affecting it closer to the trajectory's origin. Ultimately, by focusing on the origins of the attacker's strength—at his center and root—we need not move as fast as his attacking limb since that is not the object of our focus.

Training the Mind's Eye

The "mind's eye" is the way we perceive the outside world in relation to ourselves. In taijiquan we alter the normal perception via the way we practice. In doing the set slowly and with full intent, we become aware of the transition of the movement through time and create our own internal division of time according to the flow of taiji movement. Although the movements may be done quickly, this internal division of time still applies because it was previously set at a slower pace. Movements made quickly still appear to have a slow-motion quality when seen through the internal "mind's eye," allowing one to function at high speed without losing perception due to it.

Much of how we perceive time, space and movement is determined by how fast that information reaches the seat of our consciousness. If our attention is divided, external stimuli, even if slow moving, will appear quick and catch us by surprise. Fear and discomfort are two major causes of such internal noise that clouds our ability to perceive real time. Hence, there is the requirement for martial arts practitioners to develop a clear mind. By calming ourselves, sinking and relaxing to reduce tension and discomfort, losing our ego to put aside the fear of loss, we can see what is coming much more clearly. The quick is no longer that quick because one knows where it's coming from and going to and when it will arrive.

Point Focus in *Jing* Generation

Taijiquan techniques are manifested by having the qi in the body's meridians power the muscles. According to Chinese medical theories, qi is what gives the muscles the tenacity or tonus to manifest the techniques using the bones as a base. Qi originates at *yong quan* (called "bubbling well," the place where qi is stored; point K-1) and travels through the meridians causing the muscles to be qi-filled. Qi is directed by a mental focus, which is why there is the saying that the "mind leads the qi." The resulting muscular tenacity is what gives the "five bows" of the body (i.e. the back, which is the main bow, and the four limbs which are the secondary bows) the stored potential energy which can be released or shot into an opponent.

The back needs to be loose but straight to allow the unrestricted use of the muscles connected to it. Proper posture allows mental signals to pass from the nerves emanating from the spinal cord to instantaneously reach the muscles. The connecting path and the manifesting energy is referred to as *jing*. Hence, taijiquan movements are often described as "propelled." Qi is present in the body all the time, but it is its specific gathering, focus and transmission that makes it relevant in terms of martial arts.

Afterword

The above are some of the principles and practices of taijiquan. Practice according to the principles will not only bring good health but also the necessary fundamentals for application in combat. The best references for the art are still the taiji classics. Read them often and apply the principles therein to your practice. You will find as you progress that a new understanding of what they mean will become apparent. Most of all, enjoy your art and make it your very own by living and practicing it.

ENGLISH	PINYIN	CHINESE
press	an^4	按
not losing contact, not resisting	bu^4 diu^1 bu^4 ding^3	不丢不頂
sink	chen^2	沉
vigor, power, strength, energy	jing^4	勁
light sensitivity	ming^2 gan^3	明感
internal form	nei^4 xing^2	內形
gas, air, vital energy	qi^4	氣
soft hand	rou^2 shou^3	柔手
scattering hands	san^3 shou^3	散手
relax, loosen	song^1	忪
listening energy	ting^1 jing^4	听勁
push-hands	tui^1 shou^3	推手
external form	wai^4 xing^2	外形
stable, steady, firm	wen^3	穩
round, circular	yuan^2	園
mind, idea, meaning	yi^4	意
gushing spring	yong^3 quan^2	涌泉

References

Chen , W. M. (1925). *Taijiquan shu*. [The art of taijiquan]. Hong Kong: Wushu chubanshe (reprint, n.d.).

Chen , W. M. (1927). *Taijiquan dawen*. [Questions and answers on taijiquan] Taipei: Hualian chubanshe (1969 reprint).

Chen , Y. K. (1947). *Tai-chi chuan: Its effects and practical applications*. (Zhang Guoshui, Trans.). Shanghai: Kelly and Walsh, Ltd.

Chen, Y. L. (1943). *Taijiquan dao jian gan sanshou hebian*. [Taijiquan, broadsword, two-edged sword, staff, and sparring]. Shanghai: Shanghai dichan yanjiusuo.

Hsu, Y. S. (1921). *Taijiquan shi tujie*. [Illustrated manual of the postures of taijiquan]. Taipei: Hualian chubanshe (1982 reprint).

Hsu, Z. Y. (1927). *Taijiquan qianshuo*. [Introduction to taijiquan]. Shanghai: Taijiquan yanjiushe.

Lee, Y. A. (1968). *Lee's modified tai chi chuan for health*. Hong Kong: Unicorn Press.

Liang, T. T. (1977). *T'ai chi chuan for health and self defense*. New York: Vintage Books.

Sieh, R. (1992). *T'ai chi chuan: The internal tradition.* Berkeley: North Atlantic Books.

Wang, Y. Q. (1990). *Yangshi taijiquan shuzhen.* [Authentic Yang style taijiquan]. Beijing: Renmin tiyu chubanshe.

Xu, Z. J. (1991). *Yangshi taijiquan.* [Yang style taijiquan]. Beijing: Beijing tiyu yuan chubanshe.

Yang , C. F. (1931). *Taijiquan shiyong fa.* [Self-defense applications of taijiquan]. Taipei: Zhonghua wushu chubanshe (1974 reprint).

Yang, C. F. (1934). Taijiquan tiyong quanshu. [Complete principles and practices of taijiquan]. Taipei: Zhonghua wushu chubanshe (1975 reprint).

Yue, T. (1961). *Taijiquan yao suo.* Shanghai: private publication.

Zhang, Y. J. (1986). *Taijiquan li chuanjen.* [The true principles of taijiquan]. Dazhong Shuju.

Zhang, Z. X. (1993). *Taijiquan duanlian yaoling.* [Principles of taijiquan training]. Guizhou: Guizhou kexue jishu chubanshe.

Zheng, J. (1933). *Yang Chengfu shi taijiquan.* [Yang Chengfu style taijiquan]. Guangxi renmin chubanshe (1993 reprint).

Zheng, M. C. (1946). *Zhengzi taijiquan shisan pian.* [Master Zheng's thirteen chapters on taijiquan]. Taipei: Lanxi tushu chubanshe.

Zheng, X. F. (1991). *Taijiquan pu.* Beijing: Renmin tiyu chubanshe.

The Luoshu as Taiji Boxing's Secret Inner-Sanctum Training Method

by Bradford Tyrey and Marcus Brinkman

Ink rubbing of a snake and tortoise originally painted by Wu Daozi, a famed painter who lived during the Tang Dynasty (618-907). From the collection of M. DeMarco.

Within the old practices of taiji, there exists a training method that is obscure and nearly lost. This method, passed from Chen Zhangxing to his student Yang Luchan, was born out of the Luoshu, colloquially referred to as the "Magic Square."

Ancient Daoist writings reveal that there was a need to understand how and why certain celestial principles interacted to bring about change and transformation in the heavens. From out of the Great Void, an answer mysteriously appeared for all to behold. According to Chinese mythology, Yu the Great discovered a celestial and cryptic chart, the Luoshu, on the shell of a great tortoise which was emerging from the sacred waters of the Luo River.

The tortoise, appearing majestic and heavenly, embodied and represented both heaven and earth. Its back, being convex, symbolized the canopy of heaven, and the tortoise's belly, being flat, symbolized the earth. The four feet, each with four toes, symbolized the four seasons. As the seasons changed, so did the colors of the feet and toes. The colors and their corresponding seasons were said to be dark green (spring), yellow (summer), white (fall), and black (winter). Upon the turtle's body there also appeared twenty-eight constellation formations and their locations in the heavens.

The Luoshu in its most general interpretation, represents the post-heaven diagram of change. Emperor Wen was said to have found profound inspiration from the arrangement on the tortoise's shell in formulating the foundation of the Yijing (Book of Changes). In its very essence, the Luoshu is a diagram of change which evokes the positioning of the eight gua (trigrams in the Yijing).

Using a heavenly numerological arrangement, the Luoshu forms a Daoist ritual dance pattern which is drawn or envisioned upon a floor. In old taiji boxing practice, this diagram was taught as the essential element to enhance and transform the post-birth qi and spirit into a mysterious union within the practitioner. Special patterns, fistic sets, and methods of bodily motion were derived from Luoshu's pattern. While one moves within this pattern, he should regulate his breath and properly swallow the jade-dew (saliva) in order to arouse the qi and thus nourish the primogenial breath of the Inner Palace. By this means, the Luoshu is a guide to taiji boxing practice, which leads to the threshold of immortality.

The Luoshu is a divine and magical square in which the number fifteen (15) can always be reached by adding three numbers in a straight line. The arrangement is as shown below:

$$4 - 9 - 2$$
$$3 - 5 - 7$$
$$8 - 1 - 6$$

$4 + 9 + 2 = 15$	$4 + 3 + 8 = 15$	$8 + 5 + 2 = 15$
$3 + 5 + 7 = 15$	$9 + 5 + 1 = 15$	$6 + 5 + 4 = 15$
$8 + 1 + 6 = 15$	$2 + 7 + 6 = 15$	

In 1937, Chen Weiming gave an account of how his teacher, Yang Chengfu, learned a treasured lance-training process passed down to him from Yang Luchan, who had been taught this secret method by his teacher, Chen Changxing, in the Chen Village during the 1800's. Chen Weiming had also shown to many of his original students an old handwritten manuscript on taiji lance training that was compiled by him and another student of Yang Chengfu. The manuscript, complete with drawings of lance exercises, specific notes on where to move and hold qi within one's body, and how to express qi outwardly through the lance, also provided insights into why lance training, when combined with the Luoshu, is one method by which man can attain the highest excellence in corporeal form and spiritual decorum.

A manuscript of similar content was also held by Sun Lutang, according to one of his "inner sanctum" students, Jiu Hao. Jiu, a prolific researcher and writer of taiji practice, wrote that Sun's manuscript was a repository of information encompassing taiji boxing and the Luoshu, which he had compiled based on the teachings of his masters, his talks with Yang Chengfu and Yang Shaohou, his visits to the Chen Village, and personal insights into the *Yijing*. Jiu, in his teachings, explained the importance of Luoshu training in taiji, xingyi, and bagua, by giving an excerpt from one of Sun's lectures to his students:

> Through the practice of taijiquan, the yang essence is nourished and brought forth. Through the practice of taiji lance, the yin essence is aroused and enfolds. Through the union of the yang with yin, the five forces of water, wood, earth, fire, and gold come into being and merge within and throughout the body and lance. Through the Luoshu, one embarks to be inscribed upon the Register of the Immortals.

In his writings, Jiu Hao explained that Sun devoted his earliest morning hours to special forms of meditation, followed by a period of studying and interpreting the *Yijing* and its spiritual meanings and interrelations with the Luoshu. Sun then applied his interpretations to his practice of xingyi and bagua, both refining the stealth of his physical applications and cultivating himself spiritually. Jiu wrote that "Sun, over the years, changed his postures and manner of practice to be more attuned to his knowledge about qi development and his perception of the *Yijing* and Luoshu." Because these changes became so prevalent in Sun's later years, Sun remarked to his students that he practiced *bian quan* (changing fist). Some of his students misinterpreted this comment as a new fistic art that Sun had created. In actuality, Sun was referring to the significant number of changes he was making concerning postures, applications, and ways to practice. Sun wrote a book on these changes though it was said to have been stolen by a student or guest who had visited his home.

He had apparently decided not to rewrite this book. Jiu Hao, having read the book, later wrote down what he could remember, a document amounting to more than sixty pages. Jiu further annotated these pages with additional information that Sun taught. This newly compiled book on Changing Fist was later passed on to one of Jiu's inner-sanctum students.

Sun, who was well-known for his amazing feats with a lance, also wrote a text on lance practice and application that both Chen Weiming and Jiu Hao had read. This book cited numerous methods of using the Magic Square for stepping methods, lance attacks and counters, xingyi five-element lance, solo and partner training, and standing qi circulation exercises. There was also a section on lance studies applied to the Magic Square. This book, not surprisingly, was also stolen before it could be published, as was Sun's personal diary that he had written in for over forty years. Jiu Hao, once again, wrote extensive notes on Sun's lance book and accounts from the diary.

Chen Weiming wrote and published a short manuscript in Shanghai in the latter 1930's in which he explained what Yang Chengfu had been taught during one of his three-month stays in the Chen Village. The following is a partial translation:

> The Luoshu, according to many Chen family elders, is composed of both an inner and outer form, both halves embracing a myriad of meanings. The inner, in relation to the human physique, refers to the inner movement and location of qi as actuated by the five influences [elements] and the mind's will to govern the qi in movement. The outer, refers to a number of specific areas, some of which are: standing practice—in preparation for movement; combat—areas to strike and guard; and weapons—areas to focus one's attack for maiming and overcoming the opponent using lance, sword, knife, and so forth.

Chen went on to explain, based on his contact while training with certain teachers, that some schools emphasized discipline and instruction derived from their understandings of the Magic Square:

> These methods are especially taught by some of the elder teachers of the Chen taiji boxing style, Yang Luchan's original version of the Yang family art, and the Sun Lutang school. My master, Yang Chengfu, said that Yang Luchan learned both the inner and outer Luoshu applications and thus was able to attain supreme boxing skills. He passed on this knowledge to his sons, but it was Yang Jianhou who most ardently practiced his boxing according to his ever deepening understanding of the Luoshu though it was Yang Banhou, in his later years, who began teaching these guarded methods outside the Yang family circle.

The Magic Square, as applied to the exterior of the human body, is adjusted according to one's posture and purpose of practice. In taiji, bagua, and xingyi boxing arts, Magic Square principles remain identical. Briefly presented here are the five major variations of this method as outlined by lecture notes from classes taught separately by Sun Lutang and Yang Chengfu. For easy reference, Yang style drawings are used as examples.

Solo Boxing Practice

The practice of each posture must be in accord with the Luoshu. To attain such accord, one must first study the respective positions related to both the inner and outer parts of the human body and then accommodate these positions to seasonal, daily, earthly and heavenly interactions. As one comprehends both the meanings and correlations of the magic numbers, one then shall uncover the secrets of movement according to the Luoshu. One mysterious factor is the sum of fifteen.

Lance Practice

The Luoshu, in regard to lance practice, is divided into four parts. Respectively, they are the Luoshu of one's stationary body (posture), that of the body moving with the lance, that of spearing outward towards configurations of the Luoshu, and that of paired-lance practice.

Saber and Sword

In both saber and sword, the blade's angle of attack dictates the arrangement of the Luoshu. An outward thrust expands the numerical positioning, while an inward (yielding) action contracts the numerical positioning to its origin.

Two-Person Practice

As in paired-weapons practice, each person contains his own inner and outer Luoshu. When two people touch in practice, the Luoshu are said to unite between the practitioners. Changes in the positioning of the Luoshu depend upon posture, yielding, and the issuance of force at a specific point. One's success hinges upon attaining the sum of fifteen, whether yielding or overcoming.

Conclusion

The Luoshu, as one of the inner-sanctum secrets, touches upon every aspect of taiji training. Jiu Hao, in one of his visits to the Chen Village, recorded what he was taught concerning the two drawings. His recordings differ from what has been published in an old book on the Chen style which contains these same drawings. Jiu explains in his writings that "being in the presence of teachers, one is given information and insight that will not be written. The Chen family, in particular those with long beards, hold to this way steadfastly."

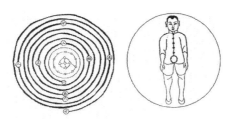

The following is an excerpt from Jiu's manuscript:

Taiji boxing's inner *jing* [force] spreads throughout the body, initiating from a single-most point. It is in a constant state of expansion and contraction. Though one is tranquil, *jing* coils as a dragon in the heavens.

Even within a single action, the *jing* is continuous from one action into another. As a spider's web, once you touch it [one's web of *jing*], you cannot escape. As in a whirlpool of water, the force swirls, and if touched, though it cannot be seen, its vortex pulls you in and no escape is possible. The *jing* has many perpetuating circular forces and though, if skillful enough, you may escape from an outer web of *jing*, you cannot escape from the center of the vortex which is limitless in its progressive strength.

Man, though in a posture inducing tranquility or in a posture of movement, has the *jing* web within and without concurrently, both reinforcing the other, as do the yin and yang. The inner *jing* and outer *jing* are likened to yin and yang. The Luoshu, having its arrangement within man's *jing* web, interior and exterior, is the heavenly thread by which all is united within the body. In this manner, the heart, the spirit, the breath, and the Luoshu may find harmonious abode in the cavity of the body, dwelling permanently within.

• 9 •

The Combative Elements of Yang Taijiquan
by Peter Lim Tian Tek

Wang Xianggen, who teaches in Hangzhou, China, topples a student.
Photo courtesy of Don Mainfort.

Other than the fact that its name can be translated as "The Supreme Ultimate Fist," taijiquan (or simply taiji for short) has always been noted as a highly effective combat art. It first became widely noted as a combat art when Yang Luchan brought it to Beijing where he taught at the imperial court. Yang was challenged many times, but no one ever came close to defeating him. So great was his skill that the martial artists bestowed on him the title "Yang the Invincible."

More recently, Yang Luchan's grandson, Yang Chengfu, promoted the art until it spread far and wide. Yang Chengfu taught his art as a combat art which can be used to strengthen the body. His three books attest to this fact. There is no substance to the widespread assumption that Yang Taiji is solely health oriented and not combat effective. By practicing taiji as a martial art, one can also gain the health benefits. Yang Chengfu, in his book *The Practical Application of Taijiquan*, wrote:

> In taijiquan, the ability to cultivate oneself physically and spiritually, but not to defend oneself, is civil accomplishment. The ability to defend oneself, but not to cultivate oneself, is martial accomplishment. The soft taiji method is the true taiji method. The ability to teach the art of self-cul-

tivation and self-defense, both cultivation and application, is complete civil and martial taiji.

– adapted from Douglas Wile's translation.

In these modern times, with the advent of modern weapons of both individual and mass destruction, the civil or health-giving aspects have been emphasized over the martial. The full art, however, as the above words explain, consists of both civil and martial aspects. One without the other is incomplete. The civil aspects of taiji have been much written about but the martial or combative principles, applications, etc. are little known and in danger of being lost.

As a martial art, taiji is very different from the hard-hitting, external martial forms. What is combat taiji then? It is certainly not about great power even though taiji is capable of generating great power. The classics state clearly that the art is not based on great power. Once, when Yang Banhou had bested an opponent and was proud of himself because of it, Yang Luchan, his illustrious father, pointed to Banhou's torn sleeve and said that he was happy that Banhou had won but did he use taiji to win? The implication is, of course, that a torn sleeve is a sign of inappropriately used power. Yang Luchan's own boxing was so soft that it was nicknamed "cotton fist" or "neutralizing fist." It was once berated as not being combat effective because of its softness, a point which Yang refuted by promptly defeating the antagonizer.

The following are some of the key elements used by taiji exponents in combat. The author and his student, WSU Taiji Club President, Desmond Tan, demonstrate some simple applications to illustrate the points discussed in this chapter.

COMBAT PRINCIPLES

A Word About Anatomical Weapons

The anatomical weapons in taiji are not rigorously hardened as in external styles of martial arts. This is because it is not hardness of the weapon but the energy within it that is the effecting component. If the correct structure of the anatomical weapon is maintained, then structurally it will be substantial and able to deliver telling blows with much power without recourse to hardening. The appropriate and efficient use of strength usually does not require great excess to obtain the desired effect. The principles behind the adage of "deflecting a thousand pounds with four ounces" hold true in taiji.

■ "Not Letting Go; not resisting"

The combat principle of "not letting go, not resisting" is first cultivated in push-hands (*tuishou*) practice and later refined in sparring hands (*sanshou*) practice. The key element in this principle is sticking (*nian*) and it operates through sticking energy (*nian jing*). This is because without sticking, one cannot "hear" the opponent's energy and its qualities and so be able to control them effectively. And, if we resist, then we give the attacker a base for which to effect his attack. That is why instead of deflecting, resisting and absorbing an opponent's attacking force, taiji exponents evade, redirect and blend with it. "Evade" means simply to move out of his way. In any attack, there are only limited points to attack, so simply removing yourself out of his attacking focus by a change of position negates it. Contact should not be a hard block, but a blending with the attacking part by yielding, sticking and following the opponent's momentum, joining his energy and redirecting it to your advantage.

Through sticking energy we can then develop listening energy (*ting jing*), which is the sensitivity to detect the opponent's strength, its origin, trajectory, magnitude and component vectors. Once we are able to detect his energy movement and center of mass, we can effectively know his intent and control it by affecting the energy flow and center of mass efficiently.

APPLICATION: Not Letting Go, Not Resisting
(A-1) Mr. Tan attacks with a left punch. (A-2) Mr. Lim, "not resisting," neutralizes the punch by leading it into emptiness. (A-3) Tan realizes he is over-extended and so withdraws. (A-4) Lim, by "not letting go," sticks to Tan, following him while adding on to his momentum and utilizes the opportunity for a push. Sequence photos courtesy of Lim Tian Tek.

■ "Following His Posture; Borrowing His Strength"

Sui ren zhi shi, jie ren zhi li simply means to follow your opponent's structure and adapt to it so that it is ineffective. This is practical application of the principle of *bu diu bu ding* by yielding and following him. Rather than a rigid application of learned postures, the applications should occur spontaneously in response to the opponent's movement.

"Borrowing his strength" is essentially utilizing the opponent's own strength against him, either by causing it to overextend or to channel it through your own body structure back to him. He is literally then hitting himself and there is little expenditure by way of energy for the taiji practitioner.

This following of the opponent's structure is first learned from push-hands, which is why it is important that push-hands not degrade into a choreographed exercise. Sensing the opponent's movements and responding to them is correct rather than just going through the motions and not sensing them. If he does not move, you should not move. Even in a static position, there will be structural flaws that can be detected by the touch, and one can attack them by moving first. But be always aware of a possible trap, even during an attack. Sensing plays a very important role in avoiding traps by responding in midattack and countering the trap.

APPLICATION: Following His Posture, Borrowing His Strength

(B-1) Mr. Tan punches, but the strike is neutralized by Lim's "ward-off" block (B-2). (B-3) Tan follows with a roundhouse kick, but Lim sticks to Tan and follows his movement by rotating and stepping forward. Lim thus redirects the power from the kick with his left arm, transfers the power into his right arm, and utilizes it to pin Tan's right arm. (B-4) Since Tan is now defenseless, Lim easily follows with a palm strike to an accupoint near the shoulder (known as *lu* 1).

■ **"Attract Into Emptiness"**

Yin jin ru kong, "attract into emptiness," is one of the most common tactics used in taiji. It is exemplified by the posture "roll-back" which implements the opponent's entry into emptiness. The tactic essentially is presenting a false target for the opponent to attack, and when he does, you spring the trap of letting his own momentum and mass be his own undoing by overextending it. Finding no target, he is naturally unbalanced and is easy to counter.

■ "Emitting Energy"

Used when the taiji practitioner attacks, *fajing* refers to the emission and transmission of energy out of the practitioner's body and into the enemy or target. The whole process is of an explosive nature, but at no point in it is the body or limbs rigid. Taiji practitioners are noted for their great power when it comes to uprooting or bouncing an opponent out. This power, however, is applied appropriately and efficiently. Having a lot of power but not knowing where to use it is quite useless; hence, the importance of sensitivity. Sensitivity allows you to know not only the opponent and avoid his power, but also to know where to apply your power to greatest effect.

So, is the appropriate use of great power then the key to self-defense? No, it isn't. Power in excess of what is required to achieve neutralization and control is inherently unstable. One must refine the process till it becomes so efficient that minimum power can produce maximum effect. Then, even an old man can best a young and strong one, not with more power but with the intelligent and efficient application of the body.

That is why masters like Zheng Manqing can send a 200-pound man flying across the room but finds a bowling ball too heavy to carry on with the sport (Lowenthal, 1991). This is no paradox once the underlying principles are understood.

■ "Long Energy"

Zhang jing (long energy) is the most common type of energy emission used in taiji. It develops from the feet, and because the energy path is long— through all the joints and ending at the fingers—it is called "long energy." It is commonly seen when taiji practitioners "bounce out" their push-hands partners. The whole body of the opponent is physically pushed away by moving his center of mass. If it is done correctly, both his feet should leave the ground when he is propelled away. This is why the technique is called "uprooting."

The energy can be developed from the rear foot, the front foot or from one to the other. All the joints in the body work coordinately and smoothly, without tension, to transfer, amplify, and focus the generated energy to the point of attack. This type of energy is usually the first to be manifested by the practitioner and, though it can be spectacular, it does not cause very serious injury.

APPLICATION: Long Energy

Long Energy (*zhang jing*) is the most common method of energy emission seen in taijiquan. It can be spectacular but seldom causes serious injury. It is often used in push-hands practice to uproot the opponent. Sequence photos courtesy of Lim Tian Tek.

■ **"Short Energy"**

Short energy emission (*duan jing*) is less common and is considered a rather advanced method. The energy transmission path is shorter than that of Long Energy and originates at the center of mass which is supported by the rooting leg. The energy emission begins at the center of mass and propagates outwards, down the root and out through the limbs. It is aimed at and acts directly upon the opponent's center of mass, using it as a base for a crushing attack that ruptures organs, rends musculature and breaks bones. The fastest application of such energy is called cold energy (*leng jing*) because the emission is so sudden that it catches the opponent by great surprise, so great that it frightens him and causes him to break out in cold sweat.

APPLICATION: Short Energy

Short Energy (*duan jing*) is directed at the center of the opponent's mass in an explosive manner. The opponent is not bounced out as with a Long Energy application, but is usually dropped on the spot.

■ **"Intercepting Energy" or "Receiving Energy"**

Jie jing skill has always been associated with the great masters and we know that Yang Luchan, Yang Chengfu, and Zheng Manqing possessed this skill. It has been said to border on the mysterious and it is hard to attain such skill. It can only be attained after one is learned in the "tenths, hundredth and thousandths" parts in taiji. At lower levels of attainment, *jie jing* is expressed mainly through the hands. At higher levels, where the entire body is responsive, it can be expressed from almost any part of the body.

With *jie jing* skill, one meets an incoming object by sticking, yielding and attaining almost the same speed as the object. This means that since the acceleration of the object and the contact point is nearly the same, their relative speed to each other is small. By "listening" to the object's center and vectors, one can apply an appropriate minimum vector to change the object's trajectory. If it is a balanced object, it can be easily pushed; if it is not, it can be easily redirected. This is what Zheng Manqing meant when he said that in *jie jing* one must first attract the object, then throw it away.

APPLICATION: Intercepting/Receiving Energy
Jie Jing can be translated both as "Intercepting Energy" or "Receiving Energy." The point of contact is the point of neutralization and also the point of counter-attack. Normally the opponent's energy has not fully reached the defender when the counter occurs. Sequence photos courtesy of Lim Tian Tek.

■ **"Tenths, Hundredths, and Thousandths Parts"**
It is possible to divide each taiji movement into ever finer gradations of movement, technique and *jing* flow. Each part is then meaningful and has an application in a combative context. The refinement of movements to efficiency is but the beginning. Later, each part of the movement has meaning, as does each part of every part, and so on.

This practice also ensures that the mind is conscious of every part of the movement and every tiny movement of the body. Sensitivity is thus trained to a very fine degree as is the response to minute stimuli. The classics state the goal quite clearly: to be so light and sensitive that "a feather cannot be added nor a fly alight."

THE FOUR ADVANCED YANG TAIJIQUAN COMBAT SKILLS

There are situations in which the skills and principles discussed above require some augmentation to make them even more effective. This situation usually occurs when the opponent's skill level is so high that an effective counter is not possible using less injurious means. In such situations, stronger discouragement is required, and to anticipate such eventualities, Yang Taijiquan has four advanced combat skills. These four skills can only be learned and applied effectively after one is able to understand each individual portion of any technique. In other words, one must be able to comprehend and put into practice the "tenths, hundredths, and thousandths parts" in taijiquan.

These four skills are recorded in the handwritten manual handed down from Yang Luchan. It must be noted that the four skills are not used entirely on their own but are integrated to form a comprehensive system of attack and defense built upon the basics of stability, sensitivity, agility and efficient use of the body and energy.

■ "Sealing Accupoints"

Bi xue, known as "hitting accupoints," is more commonly known among Chinese martial artists as *dian xue* (dotting accupoints) because the majority of these kinds of attack make use of the fingertips. Attacking accupoints is by no means unique to taiji, but the way it is done is certainly quite unique. While other martial arts often make use of serious conditioning of the anatomical weapons and vigorous body conditioning to develop the strength and resistance required to hit accupoints, taiji uses positional and structural advantage to let the opponent provide the power to hit himself with his own power and mass.

Accupoints are divided into fatal and non-fatal accupoints. Fatal accupoints are only used in a life-and-death situation as they can cause death very quickly and should not be used indiscriminately. Non-fatal accupoints are used to simply disable or incapacitate the opponent without causing too much harm. There are also accupoints that are more effective at different times of the day depending on the qi flow in the body. These timed strikes are of a more insidious nature as they are used for delayed killing or assassinations.

A sample of some of the accupoints used in taiji is provided. However, readers are advised against using them unless absolutely necessary and to refrain from experimentation as the recovery techniques should be properly understood before one practices with accupoints. Even then, it is advisable not to practice them with any sort of impact since any accupoint strike on the body is a severe disruption of the body's systems and will have both long term and short term effects on the health of the body. In most cases, even after remedial massage and accupoint treatment is carried out, herbs are taken to strengthen and stabilize the body in order to eliminate any aftereffects.

GRASP SPARROW'S TAIL

- **Wardoff (peng):** wrist and forearm points
  (LI 4/5/7/10/11, SI 6/7, Lu 5/6/7/8, H 2/3/6, P6, TW 5)
- **Rollback (lu):** wrist and upper arm points
  (TW 11/12, LI 13, P 2)
- **Press (ji):** center of chest
  (Ren 15/17, K 23, and flank, Liv 13/14, Sp 21, GB 24)
- **Push (an):** ribs (K 23, ST 19) and floating ribs (LI 13/14)

■ **"Grasping Muscles"**

Grasping musculature in taiji is akin to the specialization of *qinna* (grasping and holding), which is an advanced skill in many forms of Chinese martial arts. The difference is that in taiji, the use of positional advantage, momentum and structural advantage is of more importance than super-strong fingers. The sensitivity of combat taiji permits one to use the opponent's structure, position, mass and momentum against himself causing him to literally lock and tie himself up with his structure with the taiji practitioner simply "helping" him do it. The result of this is that the opponent becomes unstable and, therefore, vulnerable to serious injury should the taiji practitioner choose to press his advantage. The locks and holds also cause sprains, tears of the musculature and dislocations of bones at the joints, which further disable the opponent.

■ **"Sectioning Fascia"**

Sectioning fascia (*jie mo*) is directed at restricting blood flow so as to render the body ineffectual in the execution of attacks. This is done primarily by structural control so that the position and state of the musculature and soft tissues of the opponent are such that the blood flow to certain parts of the body is restricted. Blood-flow pressure points, or "gate points" as they are referred to in Chinese, are also used to effect this. This technique can cause the limb to "go to sleep" or cause a knock-out. Also part of this skill is the restriction of air flow by attacking the respiratory system and the musculature that powers it. Strikes are sometimes used to effect this.

Positional and structural advantage and use are essential to restrict and control the opponent's body. This is possible to a high degree through the tactile sensitivity attained through diligent practice in push-hands and sparring hands.

Xia Tao (L), President of the Hangzhou Wushu
Association, practicing push-hands with Jiang Jialun.
Photo courtesy of Don Mainfort.

■ **"Holding Vessels"**

Holding vessels (*na mai*) refers to the grasping, holding and pushing of the qi meridians and accupoints with the purpose of disrupting and controlling the qi flow in the body. This technique impairs the body's function and movement, thus rendering the opponent vulnerable. Whereas grasping muscle attacks the physical structure of the body and sectioning fascia attacks the circulatory system, holding vessel attacks the internal vital-energy flow, which is distinct from the accupoints and the striking of them.

110

Good knowledge of the body's qi meridians is necessary as is the results of their disruption and blockage. As with the above skills, the opponent's own body and energy are used against himself through superior information via tactile sensitivity and appropriate and efficient application to obtain the desired result.

Healing and Harming

The knowledge and skill to cause destruction and death of the body can also be used to restore health and prolong life. The four advanced skills mentioned briefly above all require a thorough and intimate knowledge of the body and its functions. This knowledge can be used to heal injuries and cure illnesses by opening blockages to qi and blood circulation, restoring proper musculature position and function.

Often, this healing function is learned first before the harming function is taught. This ensures a proper disposition and respect for the skill as well as firm grounding in the theoretical base and its practical application. It is because these skills are so destructive that they are seldom taught and many practitioners of the art are not aware of their existence. They are passed on only to the most trusted of disciples who will not abuse them but use them for the benefit of all mankind.

The Taijiquan Martial Artist

Above all, taiji exponents are encouraged to be moral people. A sense of righteousness, chivalry, kindness, compassion, nobility and being a benefit to society should always be the code of conduct for the taiji practitioner. A practitioner should embody the principles of his art and apply its stratagems and philosophies in his dealings with all things.

The aim of taiji as a martial art is to stop violence conclusively without recourse to more violence. Most of the time, violence is redirected against itself or rendered ineffectual. Hence, taiji practitioners usually overpower their opponents by just turning their own violence against themselves, educating them rather than hurting them. Violence begets violence. In taiji practice, violence is shown to act against itself. By employing taiji theory in self-defense, the destructive cycle is broken and a more rational, less confrontational solution is found to be the most effective.

Can taiji be used as an attacking art? Yes, but violence should only be the last recourse, never the first. Ego has no place in taiji as it gets in the way of efficient practice and usage of the art. Taiji itself is an art to prolong life, in peace and in combat. In practicing taiji as a combat art, peace is learned and cherished. We learn the art that we may never have to use it. With the knowledge of violence and its consequences, we choose to avoid the destructive path.

English	Pinyin	Chinese
not letting go, not resisting	bu^4 diu^1 bu^4 ding^3	不丟不頂
following his posture	sui^2 ren^2 zhi^1 shi^4	隨人之勢
borrowing his strength	jie^4 ren^2 zhi^1 li^4	借人之力
attract to emptiness	yin^3 jin^4 ru^4 kong^1	引進入空
emitting energy	fa^1 jing^4	發勁
long energy	chang^2 jing^4	長勁
short energy	duan^3 jing^4	短勁
intercepting/receiving energy	jie^1 jing^4	接勁
sealing accupoints	bi^4 xue^2	閉穴
grasping muscles	zhua^4 jin^1	抓筋
sectioning fascia	jie^4 mo^2	節膜
holding vessels	na^2 mai^4	拿脈

References

Lowenthal, W. (1991). *There are no secrets: Professor Cheng Man-ch'ing's t'ai chi ch'uan*. Berkeley: North Atlantic Books.

Wile, D. (Trans.). (1983). *T'ai-chi touchstones: Yang family secret transmissions*. Brooklyn, NY: Sweet Ch'i Press.

Chen and Yang Taiji Converge in Hangzhou City
by Donald Mainfort, M.A.

All photographs courtesy of D. Mainfort.

Introduction

Many people practice taiji as a form of gentle exercise or meditation but lack an understanding of the martial principles upon which the art was designed. However, there are several pockets of taiji enthusiasts in China where serious investigation of taiji's martial art applications is still to be found. Hangzhou is a city rich in culture and scenic beauty. There are various taiji organizations and experts in Hangzhou, but one organization in particular places great emphasis on the research and development of taiji applications. Mr. Dai Peisu and Mr. Zhang Youquan, two of the senior members of the Hangzhou Wushan Taijiquan Society, have offered to provide an introduction to their findings thus far.

Hangzhou Wushan Taijiquan Society

Mr. Dai Peisu and Mr. Zhang Youquan have been friends for many years and have exchanged information and experiences with fellow members of the Hangzhou Wushan Taijiquan Society in Zhejiang Province. Mr. Zhang is the vice president. Both he and Mr. Dai initiate contact with other practitioners and attempt to compile and evaluate the information obtained. The member-

113

ship consists of approximately sixty-eight regular local members and a handfull of overseas practitioners, mostly from the U.S. and Germany. Among the more noteworthy associates who have influenced or shared their knowledge with the group are Wang Peisheng, Yu Zhijun, Yu Tonghe, and Gao Zhuangfei, all from Beijing; Liu Chengde from Shandong; and Lin Mogen from Sichuan. Dai Peisu, Zhang Youquan, and the society's president, Mr. Xia Tao, believe that these men all have genuine skill and understanding of taiji.

Xia Tao, President of the Hangzhou Wuchan Taijiquan Society.

Dai Peisu's Taiji Studies

Dai's primary teachers were Wang Zhuocheng and Wang Xianggen. Wang Zhuocheng, who worked as a bodyguard in his youth, went on to establish a good restaurant business in Hangzhou and live a comfortable life. His neighbor, Tian Zhaolin, relied entirely on teaching taiji for his livelihood and frequently had trouble making ends meet. The two became close friends and shared their martial arts information. Wang Zhuocheng taught bagua to Tian and saw to it that his friend never went hungry.

Although Tian Zhaolin was widely rumored to have been a student of Yang Chengfu, and there are some published photos of them together, Tian's real teacher was Chengfu's father, Yang Jianhou. Tian spent some time with Yang Chengfu after Jianhou's death. Although he was remotely linked to Jianhou through his teachers, Dai said that his form was not a hand-me-down from this relationship. Rather, he said that it evolved as a result of many different teachers and influences, including bagua (also learned from Wang Zhuocheng) and xingyi. Dai learned xingyi from a master who came to Hangzhou from Shanghai who was known to him only as "Master Lin." Dai said that Lin had a deep affect on his approach to martial arts. He said that with gongfu, as with math or physics, it really doesn't matter where you get information; the principles are pretty much the same.

Wang Xianggen was born in Suzhou but has spent the latter half of his life in Hangzhou. He studied with Huang Yuanxiu, a prosperous and affable Hangzhou martial arts aficionado whose long list of friends included Yang Chengfu. Huang Yuanxiu was an intellectual and imparted some important points to Mr. Wang on how to issue power. Mr. Wang also learned Chun Yang Style Wudang sword from Huang Yuanxiu, who learned it from Kuomintang General Li Fangsen (also known as Li Jinglin). The two of them published a book entitled, *How To Exercise Wudang Sword* (1931) in Shanghai.

Although Dai Peisu views Yang Taiji as his major focus, he considers his form to be somewhat of an amalgam. People viewing his form sometimes remark: "That's not Yang Taiji! He's using a function from Wu Style there, and that's an application from Chen Style!"

Mr. Dai explains that, as most students realize, the Wu family learned taiji from Yang Banhou, so if you practice Wu style, you are, in effect, practicing a version of Yang Taiji (DeMarco, 1992: 23; Ma and Zee, 1990: 8; Wile, 1996: 35; Wong, 1996: 27, 248). Also, because Yang Luchan learned taiji from Chen Changxing, there must be a strong relationship to Chen taiji (DeMarco, 1992: 20; Zhaohua, 1984: 7-8). Before the popularity of Yang Chengfu's form (now in common use as an exercise), more of the older influences were apparent. Dai said that Yang Chengfu came to Hangzhou (Wile, 1983) and that Yang's form was deceptively simple in appearance. In fact, he was using some of the waist movement seen in earlier forms (vertical circling as well as horizontal), but did so in a less obvious manner.

Xingyi uses vertical circling to generate force and Dai Peisu incorporate this into his actions as well. When asked what form of taiji he practices, he smiled broadly and replied: "Dai's taiji!"

Dai strongly suggests that every serious student of Yang taiji should also look at the Wu style. He feels that many subtleties that seem to have disappeared in the modern teaching of the Yang style can still be found in the Wu. The small and concentrated circling actions in the Wu form were derived from the Yang's. After students practice for some time on a large frame, they should refine and concentrate their movements. He feels that Wu taiji might be difficult for beginners, though, and suggests learning the larger Yang form first until you begin to get the idea of the applications. After you see how taiji is used in self-defense, the meaning of this idea of smaller movements becomes clear.

Zhang Youquan's Taiji Studies

Mr. Zhang's primary teacher was Hong Junshen of Shandong, from whom he learned the silk-reeling method and Chen Taiji. Earlier Zhang had learned *Xiao ia* (small frame) Chen Taiji from Chen Lijing, a descendant of the Chen family from Xi'an. Zhang's first teacher was Jiang Yukun, from Beijing. Zhang says his major focus is silk-reeling along with the concept of "hardness contained in softness." Using small and compact movements to initiate explosive *fajing* and *doutan* ("trembling energy"), Mr. Zhang's form appears nebulous and it is difficult to recognize any of the set patterns that Chen Taiji practitioners are familiar with. You can see an example of this (as well as Dai's form) demonstrated in the videotape, *Taijiquan at West Lake* (1993).

Zhang approaches taiji movement as that of a clock mechanism: the small activates the larger, generating from the center, with each part following a circular pattern of hand and body. His hands are the key and they activate a chain of relationships: hand to wrist, wrist to elbow, shoulder, back, waist, legs, and finally feet. Using many joint-locking techniques (in taiji, not Shaolin style), Zhang can cause an opponent to loose his balance, which will leave him vulnerable to a whole host of explosive attacks. Zhang uses the method of *yin dao shu*, or "imaginary pathway." Here, you imagine your root of power to be somewhere else. For example, if you want to use power in your wrist, you imagine that you are actually using your elbow. If you want to use force from your elbow, you focus attention on your shoulder, and so on. The very subtle circling actions of his fingers exert astounding torque and leverage when he applies them in qinna-type situations. Zhang used the image of wringing water out of a wet towel to describe this procedure. The ease and power are much greater than those of the Shaolin qinna that I have experienced with many other practitioners around China, which were also effective, but not nearly as efficient.

Taiji Synthesis

Although he can use the explosive force of Chen taiji to do great harm, this is used only for demonstration and then only with care. Mr. Zhang prefers to use the torque of his silk-reeling to control an opponent using the smallest amount of force and causing the least amount of pain necessary. Zhang and Dai never try to hurt people, or to throw them to the ground. In practice, when they "bounce someone out," they always maintain contact so that the person does not fall. Also, they never issue harsh *fajing*, except in controlled situations

116

with advanced warning—never suddenly during friendly practice. Although Dai is known to be very expert in the issuance and neutralization of *fajing*, he differs from Zhang in that he considers this to be more in the realm of regular gongfu and not sophisticated taiji, which emphasizes soft power. Both evaluated my own attempts at issuing *fajing* and explained that most of my force was being directed into the ground, rather than into my hands. If you are making a lot of stomping noise with your feet, then you are losing your force and you will not be able to get the electrifying whip-like blast from your hands. When Zhang demonstrates it I can barely see any movement in his waist and practically none in his knees. The movement should be small and compact and the upper body should be very relaxed. It takes a proper understanding of relaxation and much practice to get good at it.

Dai said that while it is easy to become relaxed practicing the taiji solo form as a type of meditation, the goal of taiji is not just to become relaxed, but to most effectively resolve conflict in the real world. His taiji uses relaxation to enable the whip-like speed and economy that is impossible if the muscles are tight and stiff due to the "fight or flight response."[1] He said that taiji is not a process of thinking about your own relaxation, but rather one of sensing and responding to another person's actions in a creative way. In fact, it is incorrect and in violation of Daoist philosophy to become too relaxed—there must be strength contained within the softness. Sometimes when I practiced push-hands with Dai, he appeared to be less than relaxed. When I attacked his "hardness," I found that he was simply giving me an empty target and therefore my attacks fell on nothing. He also demonstrated for me how it is not good to be too relaxed on the outside in neutralizing, and that knowing this can prevent a spontaneous counterattack. Sometimes I find that when practicing with them, I am unable to move and they are just standing there, seemingly motionless, smiling at me. Then I will gradually and incrementally be set off-balance. "How do you do this?" I asked. They directed my attention to an area known as the *ming men*, in the lower back.

Both of them have highly developed musculature in this area that they can control in an undulating motion. It was very odd to see this and to feel the effect of power channeled in this way from the waist, shoulders, and out through the hands. Both Zhang and Dai advise that people breathe naturally when practicing taiji. After a while, your breathing (*tuna*) becomes naturally coordinated with certain actions. This can be taught by a proper teacher, but they warn that today most of this knowledge has been lost and they do not know anyone who has a real understanding of it. According to them, there is

117

a lot of false information being disseminated that can be harmful. The last time I spoke with Dai, he was experimenting with a method of "gulping" in air during a very fast neutralize and pull-down defense.

Mr. Dai and Mr. Zhang are close friends, yet a typical encounter with the two always results in heated debate regarding various aspects of taiji: What is practical in a real encounter? What is the role of fajing? How does the action in question reflect the principles of taiji philosophy? Are some famous classic quotations about taiji true, or are they merely clichés? There is usually a conclusion reached regarding the point in question. Many times I have heard them discuss how aspects of the form are merely gross exaggerations that are far removed from any practical, spontaneous response to an opponent. The bottom line is always "what works." They say that constant debate and critical evaluation are useful to continued discovery and improved understanding. Their debates are always accompanied by much practice, with each attempting to demonstrate the validity of his position. They are always open to new ideas or opinions and are eager to put them to the test. They feel that openly exchanging knowledge will lead to higher levels of understanding.

They encourage students to meet as many different teachers as possible and gain from varied perspectives. I attended several of the Hangzhou Wushan Taijiquan Society meetings and it was really inspiring to be able to see a variety of experts exchanging ideas and holding up their skills and abilities to peer review.

Dai once told me that Mr. Zhang was more experienced and knowledgeable about taiji than he was. Zhang responded by saying that when he first met Dai years ago, he found that Dai didn't have a clear understanding of how to maximize power from the feet. "After I explained it to him, he combined it with what he already knew and now he is better than me.... I don't care, though, because we are good friends!" Zhang said that some teachers wish to maintain an air of authority by not revealing all of their information to their students. He feels that this attitude contradicts Daoist philosophy and is harmful to taijiquan's future.

Conclusion

What I have noticed about Dai Peisu and Zhang Youquan is that although they have different styles, they are equally effective. As two accomplished painters approach the same scene in different ways, each serious taiji practitioner must determine what is effective, what works for them. Serious practitioners should eventually develop their own "style." Otherwise, taiji loses its meaning and degenerates into a kind of synchronized dance performance. For those who wish to practice taiji for health, it is necessary to understand some of the theory and practice of the applications so that your posture will be correct. Good gongfu equals good health.

Dai and Zhang both seek the balance of defend and attack (yin and yang), all in the same motion with minimum force. Each uses a different style to accomplish this, but both adhere to taiji's general principles.

What effect are you trying to achieve? Is there a lighter, more efficient way? The classics tell us that we should practice taiji by using our minds. Dai and Zhang say that the form and tuishou practice are not ends in themselves, but merely training exercises that people should not follow blindly. They are constantly seeking more sophisticated methods and they are not satisfied with ideas that cannot be proven, or that contradict Daoist philosophy.

Wang Xianggen says that the principles of Daoism and taijiquan are simple physics and should not be made complicated by mysticism. Although they say that in the beginning it is necessary to understand "hard" force (they recommend a study of Shaolin for this), the eventual aim should be to avoid any direct conflict or "meeting force with force," and that this idea has deep cultural roots in China. Mr. Zhang also points out that if you really wish to understand taiji, it is necessary to learn about some of the other traditional arts of China, such as brush painting; music; poetry; and his specialty, literature.

Both men cherish the martial art applications contained in taiji and view them as a unique part of the cultural and historical heritage of China. They also view taiji as a form of self-cultivation and as a way to reduce conflict and anxiety in daily life. Dai Peisu and Zhang Youquan say that they still have many questions regarding taiji and that taiji is a never-ending process of discovery and self-realization.

TECHNICAL SECTION

THREE EXAMPLES OF YANG TAIJI

Xie Fei (diagonal flying)

A-1: Dai Peisu's right hand uses *lu* (neutralizing action) and *chai* (pull-down action) to break his opponent's balance in such a way that his body inclines forward. Simultaneously, Dai cross steps with his right foot half a pace so that it becomes vertical to his opponent.

119

A-2: Dai steps forward with his left foot in a circular manner until it reaches behind his opponent's back, while at the same time Dai's left hand rolls forward along the opponent's chest. Strength is directed outward though the index finger, creating the action known as *peng* (wardoff). As a result, the opponent bends his back and his center of gravity is elevated.

A-3: When Dai's left arm has become tightly stuck to his opponent's body, Dai utilizes *kao* (shoulder-strike action). Remember that "shoulder strike" is an expression and the power generates from the feet, legs and waist. In the fraction of a second in which this is accomplished, Dai's right hand quickly exerts *an* (push downwards) in a backwards, arching motion and Dai's legs subsequently assume a "bow and arrow" stance.

Xie Fei method is now completed and as a result, the opponent loses his balance and falls down. Either that, or he stumbles backwards in such a way as to cause his arms to "flap," similar to the wings of a bird. This is the reason for the name of this form. Those practicing this form should not have the sense of flying—they should have a feeling that their imaginary opponent is sent flying!

One very important point to remember is that the action of the "empty arm"—it's downward, arching motion—is a key to this technique. The "empty arm" activates much of the force generated here. It creates the momentum needed to send the opponent back, along with a short, swift opening of the thighs of about an inch or so, also triggered by the action of the "empty arm."

Shan Tong Bei (spread the fan)

B-1: Using *peng* (wardoff action), Dai raises the incoming hand upwards and forwards.

B-2: His left hand passes beneath the opponent's arm pit as Dai steps forward with his left foot in the same manner as seen in A-2.

B-3: Dai's right hand quickly moves forward using *ji* (pressing action) and weighs down using *an*. This completes the form known as *Shan Tong Bei*. Note that Dai is holding the "opponent's" hand to prevent him from falling down and hitting his head. In dealing with a real opponent, you must also be careful to control the hand and arm because your head is vulnerable to his possible attack.

Ban Lan Chui (step forward, deflect downwards, perry and punch)

C-1: Mr. Dai's forearm rolls inside-out using *peng* to deflect the opponent's attacking hand.

C-2: Using *lu*, Dai neutralizes the attacking hand and cross-steps half a pace, forming an angle that is perpendicular to the opponent's feet.

C-3: Dai steps forward with his left foot in the same manner as seen in photos A-2 and B-2. At the same time, his left arm is brought straight across the opponent's chest and Dai's left hand then exerts *peng* and *ji* into the opponent's chest, locking him into position. Note that strength is extended from the index finger of the attacking hand.

C-4: Dai's right hand quickly forms a fist and strikes forward, while his legs form a "bow and arrow stance." Note that he is not attempting to strike the opponent's body with his fist. Instead, he strikes the air. There are two reasons for this. The first is that he will not receive resistance and counter-action. Second, the momentum generated from striking into the air will magnify the strength that Dai wishes to use from his waist in the form of *ji* and *kao*. This will cause the opponent to deflect and fall down.

In the three forms illustrated above, Mr. Dai avoids the hard attack, while striking the invisible, thus weak, points. His strength is not directed at the opponent's body. Instead it aims at weak points which his opponent can not easily protect, using strength from different sources in his body.

THREE EXAMPLES OF CHEN TAIJI

Jin Gang Dao Dui (immortal pounds mortar)

D-1: The opponent grabs hold of Mr. Zhang's wrists.

D-2a: Zhang keep his hands still, while at the same time loosening his shoulders and allowing the opponent to do as he pleases. Zhang then rotates his body clockwise and transfers the strength to both his hands.

D-2b: Zhang's right hand forms a fist, which is then placed in his left palm.

D-3: Zhang raises his hands up towards the opponent's head, raising his own left foot at the same time.

D-4: Zhang's hands stick to those his opponent's and he steps with his left foot beside the opponent's left foot.

D-5: Zhang circles his arms upwards and toward the left (counterclockwise) and as a result, the opponent is under control. If he continues turning, the opponent will stagger and fall backwards.

Liu Feng Si Bi (six seal, four close)

E-1: The opponent seizes Zhang's right wrist with his right hand.

E-2a: Zhang's right hand circles upward (clockwise) while his left hand gently covers the opponent's right elbow.

E-2b: Detail of hand positions.

E-3: Zhang continues circling his right hand while revolving his left hand along the opponent's right elbow (counterclockwise) then steps forward one pace with his left foot, placing it beside the opponent's left foot. The opponent's right arm is now stuck and under Zhang's control.

E-4: Zhang continues circling his right hand clockwise until the palm is downwards while at the same time his left hand continues to circle counterclockwise, so that the opponent is unable to move.

E-5: If Zhang continues to circle his body to the right, then the opponent's body will be twisted and he will fall down.

Shan Tong Bei (spread the fan)

F-1: The opponent catches Zhang's right wrist with his right hand, or he forms a right fist and strikes toward's Zheng's chest.

F-2a: Zhang loosens his shoulders and puts weight down on the opponent's wrists while his right hand revolves clockwise towards the right and the left hand secures the opponent's wrist from underneath.

F-2b: Detail of hand position.

F-3: Zhang's hands continue to revolve and raise the opponent's right hand.

F-4: Zhang keeps his hands still and turns his body clockwise to the right by turning on his left foot while stepping backwards with his right foot, placing it to the side and slightly behind the opponent's right foot.

F-5: As a result of Zhang's repositioning, the opponent's arms are twisted toward his back and his body bends backwards while his feet "float." If Zhang keeps his hands still, loosens his waist, and adjusts the rotation of his body, the opponent will remain under his control.

125

GLOSSARY

Pinyin	Wade-Giles	Character
an	an	按
cai	ts'ai	採
Chen Changxing	Ch'en Chang-hsing	陳長興
Chen Liqing	Ch'en Li-ch'ing	陳立清
Dai Peisu	T'ai P'ei-su	蝕培粟
doutan	tou t'an	抖彈
fajing	fa ching	發勁
Gao Zhuangfei	Kao Chuang-fei	高壯飛
Hong Junsheng	Hung Chun-sheng	洪均生
Huang Yuanxiu	Huang Yuan-hsiu	黃元秀
ji	chi	擠
Jiang Yukun	Chiang Yu-k'un	蔣玉坤
kao	k'ao	靠
Li Jinglin	Li Ching-lin	李景林
Liu Chengde	Liu Ch'eng-te	劉成德
Lin Mogen	Lin Mo-ken	林墨根
lu	lu	捋
ming men	ming men	命門
peng	p'eng	掤
Tian Zhaolin	T'ien Chao-lin	田兆麟
tuna	t'u na	吐納
tuishou	t'ui shou	推手

126

Wang Peisheng	Wang P'ei-sheng	王培生
Wang Xianggen	Wang Hsiang-ken	王祥根
Wang Zhuocheng	Wang Chuo-ch'eng	王卓誠
Xia Tao	Hsia T'ao	夏濤
Yang Banhou	Yang Pan-hou	楊班候
Yang Chengfu	Yang Ch'eng-fu	楊澄甫
Yang Jianhou	Yang Chien-hou	楊健候
yin dao shu	yin tao shu	引導術
Yu Tonghe	Yu-T'ung-he	余桐和
Yu Zhijun	Yu-Chih-chun	于志均
Zhang Youquan	Chang Yu-ch'uan	張幼泉

Note

[1] The "flight or fight response" is a natural response in humans and animals. In times of danger the response is automatically activated and hormones, including adrenaline (epinephrine), are released into the blood stream. These hormones help the body prepare either to stay and fight the danger or to run away from it. This is the body's normal response to danger (Benson, 1990).

Bibliography

Benson, H. (1990). *The relaxation response.* New York: Avon.

DeMarco, M. (1991). The origin and evolution of taijiquan. *Journal of Asian Martial Arts, 1*(1): 9-25.

Ma, Y., and Zee, W. (1990). *Wu style taichichuan push-hands.* Hong Kong: Shanghai Book Co.

Mastadon Productions. (1993). *Taijiquan at West Lake.* Chicago, IL: Mastadon Productions. Video series in four volumes.

Wile, D. (1983). *Tai-chi touchstones: Yang family secret transmissions.* Brooklyn, NY: Sweet Ch'i Press.

Wile, D. (1996). *Lost tai-chi classics from the late Ch'ing dynasty.* Brooklyn, NY: Sweet Ch'i Press.

Wong, K. (1996). *The complete book of tai chi chuan: A comprehensive guide to the principles and practice.* Shaftesbury, Dorset: Element Books, Ltd.

Yang, C. (1974). *T'ai-chi ch'uan shih-yung fa* (Self-defense applications of tai-chi ch'uan). Taipei: Chung-hua wu-shu ch'u pan she. First published in 1931.

Zhaohua Publishing House (compilers). (1997). *Chen style taijiquan.* Beijing: Zhaohua Publishing House.

• 11 •

The Nature of Rooting in Taijiquan: A Survey
by Stuart Kohler, M.Ls.

Introduction

As essential a concept as it is usually taken to be, the nature of root (*gen*) remains surprisingly undiscussed if not mysterious in the literature of taijiquan. From the perfectly simple description, "the root is at the feet," in the Yang tradition *Classic of Zhang Sanfeng* (Yang, 1991: 213) to the statement in the Chen tradition classic by Chen Xin, *Illustration of Taijiquan*, that one must "grip the ground with the toes" (Yan, 1997: 8), it would seem that the exact nature of discovering and developing root is either beyond words or so obvious that it need not be discussed.

Being unwilling to accept either position, the author intends in this chapter to report what may be found in the literature of taijiquan, with the ultimate goal of perhaps stimulating in-depth study by scholars and experts. Such study, arriving at a consensus of opinion, would be of great value to students of taijiquan, both novice and advanced.

Overview: The Relaxed Foot

At its most basic presentation, there appear to be two contradictory definitions or descriptions of root. The first, predominantly a Yang tradition concept, is that the root is formed at the *yongquan* or "bubbling well" point, also known as Kidney 1, located on the sole of the foot, just behind the ball of the foot. In this tradition, root is formed or enhanced by 'opening' this point to allow earth energy to rise into the body or to allow negative energy to drain from the body, particularly in traditional standing meditation posture (*zhan zhuang*). The activation of this point is accomplished by relaxation (*song*) and having the foot basically splay out as it relaxes into better and better contact with the ground. The weight is to be equally distributed around the sole of the foot (Diepersloot, 1995: 25). However, the *yongquan* points do not usually touch the ground due to the natural arch of a healthy foot. A minor variation of this view is to place the location of the specific point slightly further back, in the center of the arch of the foot (Wallace, 1998: 79).

Students are often told to employ the mental imagery of tree-like roots emanating from their feet as they relax and deepen their root for both martial and health purposes (e.g., Chuen, 1991: 31). A distinction is often made between these two, between being deeply sunk into the earth in a manner that is nearly immovable and being securely rooted in a manner that maintains a flexible martial position. Descriptions of rooting for health may seem to encourage a deep root that is unconcerned about the classical recommendation that in every movement "every part of the body is light and agile."

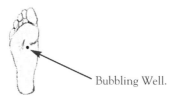

Bubbling Well.

Gripping Toes

In contrast to the relaxed foot idea is the second concept, mostly found in Chen tradition (although there are occasionally references in the Yang tradition as well [Smalheiser, 1996, December: 10]), of achieving the root by gripping the ground with the toes. Within this tradition, there ranges a variety of opinion of exactly how this is to be done, from a slight but actual physical flexing of the muscles of the foot (Montaigue, 1995: 9) to a strictly mental flexing that does not activate foot musculature, but stresses relaxation (Ting, 1996; Smalheiser, 1996, December: 10).

Ting Kuopiao offers an interesting extension to the 'gripping' description. Applying this concept to movement, he writes:

> Every motion in [taiji] originates from the feet. By moving the feet, one can maintain optimum balance, allow the whole body to move together, and gain maximum force. Moving from the feet increases speed and flexibility; we call it cat walking.

When a movement requires a step in another direction, most people simply push from the foot carrying their body's weight. But moving from the feet is a completely different concept. For example, in order to advance, as soon as the front foot contacts the earth, its toes grab the ground and pull forward. At the same time, the stationary foot pushes, moving the body's weight forward.

In other words, it is as if one pulls the body's weight forward with the lead foot, and at the same time the rear foot pushes the body in the same direction. It is important to emphasize that moving with the feet cannot be effective if all [taiji] principles are not used throughout the motion.

– Ting, 1995: 18

A more Western example of adding pulling to pushing to increase efficiency is found in bicyclists who add toe clips to the pedals. This enables them to create power strokes out of upstrokes as well as downstrokes.

Note on the Body's Integration

It should be noted that root is not solely a matter of the foot. In particular, if the upper body is stiff or disconnected, a solid root is not possible regardless of how the feet are used. For example, the *Zhang Sanfeng Classic* says: "No part should be defective, no part should be deficient or excessive, no part should be disconnected" (Yang, 1991: 213). The classic continues: "The entire body and all the joints should be threaded together without the slightest break" (Yang, 1991: 215). Craven gives some common references on this point, writing that "The education of the foot is much more than just one point or just gripping or not gripping the ground. In the subject of health, the bubbling well is activated in different ways, but the overriding point is that the entire body must be relaxed and the lock points and tensions of the body must be eliminated one by one to get the grand circulation of force" (Craven, 1997).

The reader is referred in particular to Drill #2 in the list of rooting drills at the end of this chapter for an experiential exploration of this phenomena. Nonetheless, the particular aspect of root that is the focus of this chapter relates primarily to the use of the foot, hence the apparent disregard for the necessary integration of the rest of the body.

Another level of subtlety that merits note is further distinction of types of root. Some teachers distinguish between intrinsic root, which can be either static (*zhan zhuang*) or moving (as to remain rooted during an entire round of the form), and functional (sometimes referred to as 'responsive') root, which relates to remaining rooted while confronted by an external force (Gallagher, 1994).

Western Perspective

When viewed from a strictly Western perspective, it would seem that root would be a matter of center of gravity, balance, and/or biomechanics. On the chance then that the literature of Western science (medicine, physiology, biomechanics) might yield some insight, a brief foray was made into that body of information. However, there does not appear to be an exact Western counterpart for either the concept of root or the structure or location known as the bubbling well in non-Western literature.

As related to what is called "quiet standing" in this literature, the useful information is somewhat limited in that the standard posture for such studies traditionally involves locked knees, used to apply the model of an inverse pendulum with the ankles as the pivot point (Horstmann, 1990: 165). A closer approximation to 'taiji' posture would be what is described as the "stance phase of gait" (Oatis, 1988: 1). The investigations of the biomechanics of walking and running offer some interesting insights, particularly as regards postural control systems invoked related to functional or responsive root (Rothwell, 1994: 280), but this extends beyond the scope of this survey. As an aside, it is interesting to note that the reverse may be more true: there are ever increasing numbers of references in Western journals investigating the medical benefits of taijiquan, particularly in regard to the sense of balance in the elderly.

Analysis

Is it possible, then, to reconcile these various descriptions of root? Setting aside sectarian concerns, several authors have proposed interesting theories regarding the apparent differences in description of establishing a deep root. Jan Diepersloot advances the theory that the relaxed foot is the root for health and healing, while the 'gripping' foot is the root of issuing energy (*fajing*) (Diepersloot, 1996).

A second, perhaps more ecumenical view is that both descriptions describe the same practice and that the difference in terminology relates more to the difficulty of articulating an elusive construct. On the one hand, there is the instruction to relax, often accompanied by the instruction to remain "light and agile," i.e., to avoid a flat-footed root. Extending the relaxed foot instruction is "the weight of the feet should be evenly distributed over all the cells of the sole, as if the foot were spreading itself out and grabbing the floor slightly" (Diepersloot, 1995: 25). On the other hand is the description of "gripping the ground with the toes." However, in most instances, a statement accompanies this instruction that one does so more as a matter of intention rather than physical use of muscle contraction. There is frequent mention that while gripping the ground with the toes, it is critically important to maintain a relaxed state. Ting Kuopiao discusses this concept by saying:

> 'Gripping the ground with the toes' is a sentence from a classic Chinese book about [taiji]. However, this does not mean that the student is not relaxed while he roots himself solidly with his feet. This concept is not understood by a lot of people. They mistakenly feel that gripping the ground with your toes automatically means you are not relaxed. You must relax in order to feel deeply rooted with your feet. Your toes slightly grip the ground, body remains relaxed and if you are relaxed, you will be much more rooted.
>
> – Ting, 1996

In this sense, perhaps, it could be that the "gripping" advocates seek to avoid a misunderstanding of *song* that could lead to a flat-footed or 'dead' root (all the more understandable when the metaphor of choice changes from tree-like roots to "visualizing the legs as two piles vertically inserted into the earth" (Dai, 1997: 32). Accordingly, "gripping the ground with toes" without activating musculature could be an alternative description of a *song* foot. It would therefore be possible to appreciate the commonality of these seemingly contradictory descriptions.

It should be noted that for this interpretation to hold, one would need to accept the recommendation for an actual, physical gripping (which involves the musculature of the foot) as a literalist, almost fundamentalist, view.

One additional view of forming the root and weighting the heel bears mentioning. When pressed for the exact location of root, Master Ha Fong replied that root at the bubbling well point is more for health and root at the heel is more for martial purposes (Ha, 1996).

Erle Montaigue further discusses rooting with the weight at the heel:

> The heels are very important in grounding. In pushing the heels down into the ground, we activate the "qi entering" point called Kidney 1. This point is where the ground qi comes into the body, and it is the heels that activate it. So, when we sink into the ground through the heels, we do not think about K1 point, but rather we simply push the heels into the ground by placing all of the body weight on them.
>
> — Montaigue, 1996: 33-34

Yang Zhenduo also mentions the heel in relation to root. Of particular interest is his mention of both heel and "gripping toes":

> "Your heel," Yang said, "is like the foundation of a building as you firmly plant the heel. Then as you grab with the toes, the energy goes down to the floor and also unites with the upper body movement the minute you stabilize your heel.
>
> — Smalheiser, 1996a: 10

In the final analysis, rather than attempting to divide variations in concepts of root into separate views, the larger view of Master Ha Fong may provide the most appropriate approach in seeking the nature of root. While he did provide the information referenced above relating to locating the root, it is clear that he prefers to say root is not a matter of such effort. In fact, Master Ha counsels ignoring virtually all mental or theoretical constructs. He states, "Stand up. If you don't fall down, you are rooted. The more you stand the better your root becomes" (Ha, 1996)!

A slightly more formal presentation of the same thought may be found in an interview with Master Ha:

> Fong Ha said that by putting yourself in a standing position such as Wuji, "You are activating your own automatic maintenance system. So it doesn't matter if you have bad posture. Every single cell in your body will want to maintain itself so you can stand up straight.
>
> Therefore it is self-correcting at all times, regardless of your state of health, regardless of the state of destruction going on in your body. Your body is automatically self-adjusting and self-maintaining.

By simply doing the Wuji stance, you are activating it already. There is nothing else you have to do. In my theory, you don't have to be able to stand in any special way. Just stand up and already the work is done.

— Smalheiser, 1996b: 16

A Call for Scholarship

The subtitle, "A Survey," was carefully chosen for this chapter in that the author is only able to draw upon references found in the contemporary and popular literature of taijiquan. As suggested in the introduction, it is hoped that scholarly contributions on this topic will lead toward a deeper and more definitive understanding about the nature of root in taijiquan and perhaps in Asian martial arts in general.

ROOT DRILLS
Exploring Root Experientially

1) Horse Stance

Deliberately move the weight into the heel, feel the involvement of the quadricep muscles. Deliberately move the weight into the toes, feel the involvement of the calf muscles. Roll to the outside and inside of the feet. Then return to passing the weight directly through the bubbling well point. Feel the foot splay out. Notice the alignment of the knee does not extend beyond the toes when weight is passed through the bubbling well point (experiential confirmation of the "rule" to never extend the knee beyond the toe).

Variation: Use single-legged stances from the taiji form to explore the location of root.

2) Bow Stance/WardOff

Find the correct alignment of the spine so that a gentle push or pull is directed immediately down to the bubbling well point of the front foot. Deliberately 'break' the alignment at the waist by leaning forward just a fraction while receiving a gentle push or pull from a partner. Notice how small the amount of lean is required to completely disrupt the root. This may be taken as experiential confirmation of the line from the *Wang Zongyue Classic*, "No tilting, no leaning" (Yang, 1991: 218).

Variation: Deliberately distribute your weight 50/50 and notice how little force is required to break the root when applied to the centerline.

134

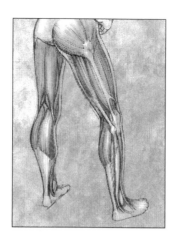

3) Bow Stance to Cat Stance

"Pour" the weight from the front foot (bow stance) into the rear foot (cat stance). Feel the bubbling well point in the rear foot, although do not ignore exploration of rooting from the heel in a rear-weighted stance. "Pour" the weight back into the front leg, directly down the shin, through the bubbling well point, into the ground. Deliberately move the weight into the heel or the toes of the front foot and notice the disruption of the root.

4) Alternating Bow Stance (as in Twist Step, Brush Knee sequence)

Pour the weight directly into the bubbling well point of the front foot with each step. Deliberately allow the weight to pour into the heel or toes and notice the disruption of the root.

Substitution of a forward shuffle step or forward triangle step may be more familiar to some martial traditions. The latter is particularly significant when exploring the idea of "pulling with the front foot" when moving forward as articulated by Ting Kuopiao (Ting, 1995: 18).

5) Wave Hands Like Clouds (one side, e.g., left)

Have a partner stand at approximately right angles to you and extend opposite arm (i.e., if you will be 'waving' your left arm, partner extends right arm, insides of wrist points toward you). Step out to the side and pour the weight into the bubbling well point; as the hand rotates across, lightly grip your partner's wrist and gently pull the partner's weight into your bubbling well point. Deliberately move your weight into the heel or toes and notice the inefficiency of your pull.

6) Bow Stance

Partner pushes gently into abdomen—keep the *dantian* soft. Staying soft permits redirection of energy into the root. Otherwise, one would be creating a false root at the *dantian* and would lose stability if the partner suddenly withdraws energy.

7) Facing Horse Stances

Each partner rests tips of fingers lightly on upper chest or shoulders of the other. Take turns applying gentle pressure to see where the pushee loses the root (i.e., is pushed back into instability).

Variation: Simultaneous gentle pushes, until one partner is pushed back into instability.

8) Dropping Into Root

Begin in horse stance, arms crossed against chest. Partner gently and steadily pushes on the crossed arms as energy is directed into the root of the feet. When the energy becomes too much for the root to withstand, drop back into bow stance, immediately "falling" into the root of the front foot.

Advanced variation: Once a bow stance is adopted, the partner continues to push until root of bow stance is broken and the root is moved into the rear foot.

9) "Receiving Energy"

An advanced drill: as your partner is just about to initiate a real push, advance slightly toward your partner while remaining completely 'sunk' (or "slid," as Paul Gallagher likes to describe it) in the energy-body and very rooted. If the timing is correct, the partner will be unbalanced backwards by the force of his or her own push.

Bubbling Well.

Note: Paul B. Gallagher (1994) provided Drills 8 and 9.

Bibliography

Chue, L. (1991). *The way of energy*. New York: Simon and Schuster, Inc.

Craven, J. (1997, June 14). Letter to the author.

Dai, D. (1997, October). How to establish a good root. *T'ai Chi, 21*(5), 32-33.

Diepersloot, J. (1995). *Warriors of stillness: Meditative traditions in the Chinese martial arts, volume 1*. Walnut Creek, CA: Center for Healing and The Arts.

Diepersloot, J. (1996, November 15). Letter to the author.

Gallagher, P. (1994, July). *Seminar on rooting*. Guilford, VT: Deer Mountain Taoist Academy.

Ha Fong. (1996, July). *Seminar on Yiquan*. Northfield, VT.

Horstmann, G. and Dietz, V. (1990, August). A basic posture control mechanism: The stabilization of the centre of gravity. *Electroencephalography and Clinical Neurophysiology, 76*(2), 165-176.

Montaigue, E. and Babin, M. (1995). *Power taiji*. Boulder, CO: Paladin Press.

Montaigue , E. (1996). *Ultimate dim-mak*. Boulder, CO: Paladin Press.

Oatis, C. (December, 1988). Biomechanics of the foot and ankle under static conditions. *Physical Therapy, 66*(12), 1815 to 1821.

Rothwell, J. (1994). *Control of human voluntary movement*, 2nd ed. New York: Chapman and Hall.

Smalheiser, M. (1996, December). Yang Zhenduo on unifying internal energy. *T'ai Chi, 20*(6), 6-11.

Smalheiser , M. (1996, June). Wuji qigong: Harvesting inner resources. *T'ai Chi, 20*(3), 14-17.

Ting, K. (William Ting). (1995, August). Fundamentals of correct t'ai chi practice, *T'ai Chi, 19*(4): 14-18.

Ting, K. (William Ting). (1996, October 16). Letter to the author.

Wallace, A. (1998). Internal training: The foundation for Chen taijiquan's fighting skills and health promotion. *Journal of Asian Martial Arts, 7*(1): 58-89.

Yan, G. and Cravens, J. (1997, April). Rooting: The secret of getting power from the earth. *Internal Martial Arts Research Newsletter*, pp. 5-9, 16-17.

Yang, J. (1991). *Advanced Yang style tai chi chuan, vol. one*. Boston: Yang's Martial Arts Association

• 12 •

The Pedagogy of Taijiquan in the University Setting
by Andy Peck, M.S.Ed.

All photographs courtesy
of Dr. Xu Tingsen.

Introduction

The landscape of universities in the United States is changing. According to the U.S. Department of Education, women will outnumber men in undergraduate and graduate programs by 9.2 million to 6.9 million by the year 2008. Not only are there changes in the make-up of gender on college campuses, but the number of students entering colleges for re-training is also on the rise. Changes in the demographics of college students also includes a higher average mean age (Koerner, 1999). These factors are coupled with a trend of decreasing physical education requirements in college curriculums.

The phenomenal growth of taijiquan (abbreviated below at taiji) during the past decade has occurred because it addresses the needs of a growing number of Americans, including college students. Taiji offers a low impact, life-long exercise, coupled with intellectual stimulation and effective stress management. This chapter will look at how one college presents taiji classes.

Background or Dr. Xu Tingsen

One taiji instructor addressing the needs of the modern college student is Dr. Xu Tingsen. Dr. Xu is eminently qualified as both an academician and martial artist. A native of Shanghai, China, Dr. Xu received his doctorate degree in biochemistry from the Academy of Medical Sciences in Moscow. He has accumulated over 43 years of experience in researching medical bio-chemistry, particularly in the areas of metabolism and cholesterol regulation. As an academic Dr. Xu has been quick to apply the scientific method to the effects of the practice of taiji. During his tenure at the Shanghai Academy of Sciences, Dr. Xu and his colleagues found that patients with high blood pressure who practiced taijiquan five times a week, while taking no medication, reduced their blood pressure by 35%. Patients who combined taiji practice with medication were able to reduce their blood pressure by 50% (Chase, 1995). As an associate professor of physical rehabilitation at the Emory University School of Medicine, Dr. Xu was awarded a grant by the National Institute of Aging (NIA) and the National Center for Nursing Research. This grant funded research to explore new ways of improving strength, mobility, balance, and endurance in people over 75 years of age. In this study, Dr. Xu and his associates found that the practice of taijiquan reduced the participant's risk of multiple falls by 47.5% (Barnhart, et al., 1996). Not only is Dr. Xu a seasoned academician but his martial arts background is equally extensive. He began his taiji training at the age of 15 and studied the Chen form of taiji under Gu Liuxin, a student of Chen Fake. He studied the Yang style under the guidance of Po Bingru, senior student of Yang Chengfu, and pursued the Wu style taiji under the guidance of Shen Renzhu, senior student of Wu Jianquan, founder of a Wu style. Dr. Xu has taught taiji in the United States for over 18 years and has been a tireless promoter of taiji. Dr. Xu has been the Executive President of the World Taiji Research Association, Beijing, and a National Advisor to the United States of America Wushu Kung Fu Federation.

Eastern vs. Western Methodologies

Traditionally in China, teachers take an interest not only in the student's academic life but also in their social and moral development, viewing the student holistically. There is heavy emphasis on past tradition and memorization. Great importance is placed upon the absorption of pre-existing facts. In class "students present themselves as attentive, respectful, and above all passive" (Grove and Hu, 1991). Self-expression and self-assertiveness are discouraged. Western approaches to teaching, on the other hand, have a tendency to attach importance to analysis and creativity rising from that analysis. More emphasis is placed upon processes than is placed on pre-existing fact. In many instances students are taught to question and challenge the a status quo. Western teachers value and appreciate student comments and input. While western teachers do show concern for their students, it is considered "unprofessional" for the instructor to address areas of the student's life not directly related to the subject being taught.

Dr. Xu's Approach

Dr. Xu attempts to employ both Eastern and Western approaches to his teaching. Dr. Xu's class however is, without a doubt, a window into Chinese culture and ways of thinking. Dr. Xu states that "in China, loyalty to a master is almost devout. American students respect the instructor but not like Chinese students, but that is understandable. Chinese students would have the same problem trying to understand American football at first." He further states that "Their [the students'] mind should be like an empty vessel waiting for the knowledge of their instructor" (Smallheiser, 1992).

The Essence and Application of Dr. Xu's Teachings

The prevailing theme of Dr. Xu's taiji instruction is that of balance. Dr. Xu emphasizes balance in the physical practice of taiji, in social relationships (including martial confrontations), and in the mental/spiritual realm as well. Inherent in the concept of balance is the premise of paired opposites or yin and yang. These opposites may manifest themselves as attack and defense, giving and receiving, expansion and contraction, pride and humility, and so on. Taiji practitioners view these paired opposites as going through cyclical changes that, like the yin and yang symbol, are changes characterized by circular, spherical or spiraling patterns of motion. In all of the practical taiji applications which Dr. Xu teaches, the principle of balance through cyclical change is evident. Movements from the traditional taiji practice of "push-hands" also embody the cyclical change of opposites.

Another characteristic of the yin-yang symbol is that a small part of one extreme is always found within the opposite extreme. Just as inhalation is about to reach its peak the potential for exhalation begins to arise. Therefore, according to Dr. Xu, even when retreating, the idea of advancing must be retained. The intermingling of the two opposites gives a unique quality to the motions of the taiji practitioner. This quality is summed up in such traditional sayings as: "resist without opposing", "yield without retreating", "relaxed but not limp" and "firm but not hard, soft but unyielding." While these sayings may sound paradoxical, there are practical applications. Occasionally Dr. Xu and his students will practice pressing on each other. In this practice those receiving the pressure learn to resist not with muscular tension but with a relaxed strength generated by specific skeletal alignment. This alignment creates a clear line of force through the body from the ground to the point of contact. Strength generated in this manner is referred to as "whole body power."

Dr. Xu's students learn to apply this principal of alignment with "whole body power" not only in static positions but in all of their motions. Guided by this inner principle they can flexibly adapt to a myriad number of unique situations.

Interviews with Dr. Xu's Students

Interviews I conducted with students of Dr. Xu's taiji class reveal what happens when western students are given a glimpse into Chinese culture and teaching methodologies. All of the students interviewed were undergraduate students of Emory University located in Atlanta Georgia. When students were asked how their classroom experience differed from the expectations they had had before beginning the class, they stated how pleasantly surprised they were to have philosophy presented both as physical motion and as a lifestyle. Dr. Xu recognizes that the western mind set is geared toward immediate gratification. On the other hand he knows that the art of taiji cannot be mastered in a matter of a few weeks or months.

While Dr. Xu transmits a tremendous amount of knowledge in a very short time span, he refuses to compromise the quality of what he teaches. The students interviewed said that the class was very detail-oriented. Yet while the class seemed to move at a slow pace, it stayed precisely on schedule as the school term progressed. Dr. Xu was careful to monitor the progress of his students. The students said that the quantity of material covered by Dr. Xu was determined by their own progress.

In terms of evaluation, the students indicated that they were critiqued and corrected in the process of learning, receiving immediate feedback on their performance. While final grades were based on the subjective opinion of Dr. Xu, all of the students interviewed felt that his evaluations were fair and even-handed. This may be related to the fact that Dr. Xu had earned the respect of his students. They stated that they trusted his experience and background and that his instruction seemed in no way "franchised."

When asked about what insights or impressions they had gained into Chinese culture, the students indicated that having a "native" teacher was very helpful. They also found the philosophy presented by Dr. Xu to be "totally different from the book type of philosophy." Dr. Xu gave them further exposure to Chinese culture by presenting the histories of each of the different taiji styles.

Finally, the students interviewed were asked about the benefits they had received from the class. The students responded by citing the following benefits. Taiji practice provided an enhanced focus of mind. They found the practice of taiji to be a natural stimulant. They indicated that their inclination to use caffeine or cigarettes to stay awake while studying was decreased. One student indicated that when he tired of his studies, a few minutes spent going through some of the basic taiji movements invigorated him, enabling him to continue his studies. Taiji was a great form of stress management and relaxation. Regular practice improved both physical and mental balance. They learned that taiji was a healthy form of exercise.

Conclusion

It is apparent from the student responses that Dr. Xu does teach taiji in a very traditional manner. At the same time attempting to cover the diverse areas of taiji in a 14 week academic semester, Dr. Xu has certainly had to make some modifications and allowances for the western approach to learning. What is also evident from the interviews with Dr. Xu's students is that taiji does address the needs of the contemporary college student. While students find the eastern perspective to be intriguing and even perhaps refreshing, they also discover practical and healthy ways to combat stress. They learn to find balance both mentally and physically. They see how a philosophy can permeate a lifestyle. They are given concepts and practices which can benefit them for a lifetime. While there may be some depth lacking due to the brevity of a college semester, university students are given a glimpse into a world they had not previously known.

References

Barnhart, H., Coogler, C., Kutner, G., McNeely, E., Wolf, S., and Xu, T. (1996) Reducing frailty and falls in older persons: An investigation of tai chi and computerized balance training. *Journal of the American Geriatrics Society 44*, 489-497.

Chase, L. (1995-96, Winter). The art of balance. *Southern Lifestyles*, 18.

Grove, G., and Hu Wenzhong. (1991). *Encountering the Chinese.* Yarmouth, Maine: Intercultural Press, Inc.

Koerner, B. (1999, Feb. 8).Where the boys aren't. *U.S. News and World Report*, 47-50.

Smalheiser, M. (1992). Tai chi and life: A search for balance. *Tai Chi, 16*(6), 5.

Acknowledgments

Mr. Peck would like to acknowledge the collaborative effort of Dr. Xu Tingsenin the writing of this chapter. Dr. Xu and his students were most supportive in providing content specifics and editorial review for this chapter.

• 13 •

A Comparison of Yang Style Taijiquan's Large and Medium Frame Forms

by Joel Stein, M.S.

Illustrations courtesy of Joel Stein.

Introduction

Classical Yang Style taijiquan (or taiji) offers three variants or "frames" within its agenda of fixed forms: the Small, Medium, and Large Frames. It is important to understand that the term "frame" does not refer to the outward appearance of postures but rather the internal movement characteristic of taiji. However, there are external as well as internal differences in each of the three frames. While much of the information about the masters and their associated forms was handed down as oral tradition, we can realize their intentions from the historical and social context in which they developed.

Yang Jianhou's Medium Frame form was a modified version of the original Chen Family Style called Old Frame (*Laojia*). The revised format helped Yang Taiji gain a considerable following. However, it was not until Yang Chengfu made additional changes that Yang taiji's popularity reached worldwide proportions.

This chapter investigates the Medium Frame form in its role as the basis for Yang Chengfu's Large Frame form by comparing the stances of both. Comparison of the Large and Medium Frame forms should shed light on the necessity of Yang Chengfu's revisions. It should also give a better understanding of the body mechanics involved in both forms.

CHARACTERISTICS OF
MEDIUM AND LARGE FRAME FORMS

Medium	Large
• Focuses on energy discharge at point of contact and centering gravity	• Focus is on *song*, opening joints, stretching tendons and ligaments,
• Martial aspects more obvious in the executed form	• Martial aspects not as obvious in the form
• Medium circular movements	• Large circular movements
• Standard base (shoulder-width) and height constant (regular) throughout form	• Standard base (shoulder-width) and height constant (regular) throughout form
• Offense/defense directed at point of contact	• Wardoff (*peng*) energy at any point
• Coiled energy emphasized	• Relaxed (*song*) energy emphasized

Background

As Yang Luchan's reputation as a peerless fighter spread throughout China, more and more people wanted to learn the style he created. The style he practiced was called "cotton boxing" or "shadow boxing." Its strength was derived from internal power rather than external force. Yang Style became the "softest" of the internal styles. However, it presented a problem in that it was a very difficult style to learn.

Yang Zhenduo comments on the progression of Yang Family Taiji dating back to Yang Luchan (1799-1872; also known as Yang Fukui):

> To meet popular needs, Yang Luchan gradually deleted from the series of movements such difficult actions as jumps and leaps, explosion of strength and vigorous foot stamping. After revisions by his third son Yang Jianhou (1839-1917), this series of movements came to be known as "Zhong Jia" ("Medium Frame"). Later, it was again revised by Yang Chengfu (1883-1936), the third son of Yang Jianhou, which finally developed into the present "Da Jia" (Big Frame) style because of its extended and natural posture, slow and even movements. It was different from his uncle Yang Banhou's style which was known under the name "Xiao Jia" (Small Frame).
>
> – Yang, 1991: 5

Yang Luchan first practiced a form known as Chen Family *"Laojia"* or "old frame." Yang Zhenduo speaks about the origins of Yang taijiquan in his book, *Yang Style Taijiquan*:

> The Yang school of taijiquan was born out of the Chen school of taiji-quan which was known as *"Laojia"* ("Old Frame"). The movements are relaxed, even and graceful like the drifting clouds and flowing stream, quite unlike the Chen style (Cannon Fist) which alternates slow and quick movements, and vigorous with restrained and controlled actions.
>
> – Yang, 1991: 5

Yang Luchan's third son, Yang Jianhou (1839-1917), revised the forms his father taught him. He omitted the hard stomps, leaps, and complex hand and foot movements. He also modified the small circular movements by making them larger and more obvious for his novice students. This revision was called the Medium Frame format. The form was somewhat easier to learn but still required the discipline and dedication of a talented student to master.

According to T. Y. Pang, Yang Luchan's third son Jianhou (1839-1917) created a medium form set and Jianhou's younger son Chengfu (1883-1936) created a new big form that became the most popular taiji style.

Yang Chengfu went on to revise the Medium Frame form by adding still larger circular movements and moving the body weight distribution further behind the front leg. He changed the weight ratio of 70/30 to 60/40 in order to shift the burden of the front leg and open the pelvic joints. These revisions, along with a viable instructive program, made Yang Style taiji popular throughout the world. Yang Zhenduo remarks about the Yang Chengfu's revisions:

> Yang Jianhou taught Yang Chengfu very seriously.... Yang Chengfu removed the vigorous *"fajing"* (release of power), energetic jumping, heavy stepping, and other difficult movements to create *"da jia"* (large frame style). *Da jia* has slow, steady, and soft movements suitable for general practitioners. The posture is neat and simple; the structure is elaborate and centrally balanced without leaning towards any sides....
>
> – Yang, 20 February 2001b

Yang Chengfu's Large Frame form became the most popular in the world. Master Vincent Chu, author of *Beginner's Tai Chi Chuan*, writes about Yang Chengfu's revisions to the form in his article, "Yang Style History":

After Yeung Ching Po [Yang Chengfu] came to Southern China, he realized that [taijiquan] was also effective in treating chronic diseases, building up one's health, and bringing longevity. When he gave [taijiquan] exhibitions in "Zhiru Wushu Association" during his early days in Shanghai . . . he performed his kicks with speed and force. Later, however, to suit the needs of chronic disease, he changed them into slow movements with inner exertion of force. And in such movements as Punching Downward and Punching the Opponent's Groin, he only made initiations instead of manifest exertions of force, thus making the movements continuous and with an even pace.... Creating a style all his own, he had mastered extraordinary skill in "*Tuishou*" or Push Hands and was good in both attack and defense.

– Chu, 12 February 2001

Characteristics of the Medium Frame

At first glance the Medium Frame form bears a striking resemblance to the Large Frame form but there are major structural differences. Both form sets are executed at the same speed and timing and the same number of movements. The Medium Frame form appears more compressed and coiled than the Large Frame form. Both the Large and Medium Frame forms have a shoulder-width standard for the base.

Overall, circular movements are smaller in the Medium Frame form. In the Large Frame form the torso is held upright and perpendicular to the ground and the rear leg is bent. In the Medium Frame form the torso is inclined forward placing more weight over the front leg. There is more emphasis on opening the joints in the Large Frame form.

Medium Frame characteristics are more apparent when we compare photos of similar postures in Large Frame form. However, it is important to note that the most significant differences in the two forms are in the movements leading up to the stances.

Generally speaking, there are no fixed or rigid applications for classic Yang taiji postures. Although certain postures are applicable to particular circumstances, they are not necessarily designed for only one specific attack or defense. The movements are flowing and flexible and they conform to the situation at hand. This holds true for both Medium and Large Frame forms.

Analysis of Large and Medium Frame Postures

Dimitri Mougdis, a senior student of Grandmaster Chu Gin Soon, is the director of the Internal Arts Institute of Hobe Sound, Florida. He believes that teaching both the Large and Medium Frame forms offers his students a more complete transmission of classic Yang taiji. The postures he demonstrates in this chapter are common to both the Medium and Large Frame forms.

In the Medium Frame Press (fig. 1), the body weight distribution is 70 percent over the front leg and 30 percent over the rear leg. The Press is sensitive to tension and is issued the instant it is detected in an opponent. In the Large Frame Press (fig. 2), the inclined torso is straightened to a 90-degree angle, redistributing the body weight to 60 percent on the front leg and 40 percent on the rear leg. The bent rear knee allows for opening pelvic socket joints (*kua*).

In the Medium Frame Fair Lady Plays Shuttles posture (fig. 3), the torso is tilted forward and the body weight is over the front and rear legs in a 70/30 percent distribution. Energy is focused and issued through the right palm. The Large Frame Shuttles posture (fig. 4) holds the torso upright with a 60/40 percent weight distribution. Striking energy is also issued through the palm at the point of contact. Although the two postures seem to be the same in outward appearance, the movements leading up to the final stances are different. Large Frame Fair Lady Plays Shuttles has large circular movements leading up to the demonstrated stance. The Medium Frame movements are compressed and coiled, the circular movements are not as obvious.

Medium Frame Wardoff (fig. 5) is both an offensive and defensive posture. The pelvic girdle is inclined slightly forward with 70 percent of the body weight over the front leg. Energy is concentrated and then issued from the left forearm when contact with an opponent is made. The Large Frame Wardoff (fig. 6) sinks the center of gravity down to the coccyx and through the legs with 60 percent of the body weight on the front leg. Energy travels from the legs (including the feet) to the waist and up through the arms and hands. It can be issued at any point of contact.

When applied, the rollback is used to pull an opponent off his center of gravity. In the Medium Frame rollback (fig. 7) stance, the head faces the direction of the forward leg with the waist at a 45-degree angle. Arms are held firmly in position and the upper body is tilted slightly forward. Although the application is the same in the Large Frame rollback stance (fig. 8), there is a more pronounced twisting of the torso at a 90-degree angle from the front foot. The upper body is held perpendicular to the ground and "sunk." This aids in opening the joints. Arms and hands are relaxed and keep the form's structure.

The Snake Creeps Down posture is both evasive and offensive. Medium Frame Snake Creeps Down (fig. 9) is a noticeably coiled posture with the upper body leaning forward and with the front leg straight. Yang Chengfu modified this posture in the Large Frame form by setting the upper body at a 90-degree angle, by having the left elbow bent. In the Large Frame Snake Creeps Down (fig. 10) the front leg is bent at the knee. This is another example of the emphasis Yang Chengfu placed on *song* or sinking the weight to open the body. In this case, the pelvic region (*kua*) and waist (*deng*) benefit.

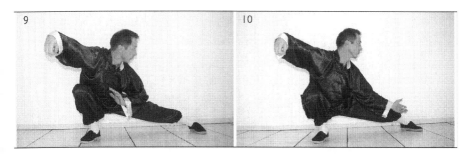

Body weight is distributed 70 percent on the front leg and 30 percent on the rear leg in the Medium Frame Single Whip (fig. 11). The left hand seems to move straight from the chest but this is actually a circular movement, which is imperceptible if not pointed out. The same movement in the Large Frame Single Whip (fig. 12) is executed with a large circular movement of the striking hand. In the Large Frame Single Whip the upper body is perpendicular to the ground. There is a slight sinking of weight (*song*) down through the coccyx/tailbone region. This sinking at the conclusion of this posture also enables the pelvic joint sockets to stretch or open.

In the Medium Frame Cross Palm posture (fig. 13), the head faces in the direction of the front foot. Seventy percent of the body weight sinks down through the front leg and the rear leg is held straight. In the Medium Frame posture the back of the right hand touches the elbow and there is a slight bend in the striking arm.

Yang Chengfu modified the angle of the waist in the Large Frame Cross Palm posture (fig. 14). The upper body is at a 90-degree angle and the rear leg is bent. The right hand guards the rib cage. These revisions allow further sinking and opening of the joints.

The Medium Frame Play Guitar posture (fig. 15) was modified to the Large Frame Raise Hands posture. In the Raise Hands posture, both palms face the opponent and the body is held upright. The Large Frame includes Raise Hands (fig. 16) and Play Guitar as part of the form.

Conclusions

Yang Chengfu modified the Medium Frame form by shifting the center of gravity in its postures. He stressed large circular movements and the sinking of body weight through relaxation. This enables novice students to open their joints, stretch tendons and ligaments, and to become more aware of their center of gravity in a more facile manner compared with the Medium Frame form.

The importance of the Yang Style Medium Frame's role in the creation of the Yang Style Large Frame form cannot be overemphasized. It provided the infrastructure from which Yang Chengfu created his revised form. The brilliant innovations helped thousands of individuals to learn the mechanics of taijiquan.

However, in its own right the Medium Frame form is an integral part of classic Yang Style transmissions. Great masters such as Yang Sau Chung (1910 -1985) practiced the Medium Frame form exclusively. And Yang Chengfu once commented that the Yang Family transmissions are not complete without it.

Acknowledgment
Mr. Dimitri Mougdis
deserves credit for
the Medium and
Large Frame poses
that appeared the chapter.

References

Chu, V. (1999). *Beginner's tai chi chuan*. Burbank, California: Multi-Media Books and CFW Enterprises.

Pang, T. (1987). *On tai chi chuan*. Bellingham, Washington: Azalea Press.

Yang, Z. (1991). *Yang style taijiquan*. Beijing: Morning Glory Publishers.

Zhang, L. (1992). *Wonderful taiji kungfu*. Henan, China: People's Physical Education Press.

Yang, Z. (20 February 2001b; download date). Introduction to grandmaster Yang Cheng-fu. http://www.yangstyletaichi.com/Home/History/Yang_Cheng-Fu/yang_cheng-fu.html.

14

Taiji Solo Form:
The Benefits of Group Versus Individual Practice
by John Loupos, B.S.

Photo courtesy of John Loupos.

"Normally, taiji practice is a solo affair, hemmed in by the frenetic pace of daily life…. Though taiji is principally an individual journey, companionship along the road is to be treasured." – Dr. Jay Dunbar

As you might infer from the preceding quotation, there is no hard and fast consensus as to the relative merits of group practice versus solo practice. When you practice taiji on your own, you are the primary variable in the experience, there being no one else to take into consideration. Of course, other considerations, such as the conditions under which you practice (terrain, lighting, weather, your most recent meal, time of day, etc.), will have some effect on any given practice session, as can your own personal subjective aspects. But, if it's just you and your taiji, the potential for unanticipated influences from outside sources is about nil.

You are alone with yourself. It's a beautiful, brisk morning as you stroll out to your lawn, or the park, or the quiet confines of whatever personal sanctum you have available. As you stand in quiet preparation, prior to embarking on one more in an untold number of repetitions of your taiji form, you feel yourself rooting to the earth. Your body automatically enacts a multitude of minor adjustments, and your respiration softens and slows as the parasympathetic branch of your autonomic nervous system prevails, relaxing you down to a deeper level. With the first moves of your form you feel any residual kinks in your body announcing their release and melting away. Soon your mind and spirit follow as internal energy (*qi*) starts to tingle through your body's energy pathways. In the whole universe, there is only you in your oneness with all, and the timelessness of the moment you are in.

Solo practice offers the opportunity to move at your own pace and with attention to your own agenda. If you have a notion to linger over this move or that for extra practice, that's your prerogative.

On the other hand, group practice offers the prospect of mingled energies, whether distractive or harmonious. When you practice your taiji with others, their presence can't not affect your experience. In fact, there are a number of reasons why practicing taiji in a neighborly way can yield benefits above and beyond what you might expect from solo training.

Whenever two or more people practice taiji together, the "energy" changes. As one member of a group, you may feel an aura of anticipation, a heightened sensitivity to the parameters of your physical space in proximity to those around you, or a peripheral awareness of timing your moves to the moves of others. Exactly how your energy changes may also depend on the specific group context. Practicing in your regular class, alongside familiar fellow students with your teacher at the helm will likely feel different from practicing with acquaintances at the park or with unknown peers at a tournament or taiji get together. Regardless of the context, group practice offers you an opportunity to learn how to engage the energy of your taiji with the energy of others who are on a similar path.

As a teacher, I have more than the usual opportunity, incentive, and responsibility to pay attention to the dynamics of group practice. Experience has taught me that any shift in energy can be used as an opportunity to learn something new and to increase one's perceptive abilities. For example, a feeling of enhanced sensitivity and refined perception are necessary precursors to synchronized timing. Synchronized timing implies your ability to match your moves exactly to the moves of others around you. Naturally, the whole issue of synchronized timing is moot if you are practicing alone. But when practicing alongside others, each person shares equally in the responsibility for keeping the group moving in unison. (Note: In actual practice, and depending on the size of the group, if novices or beginners are involved, more experienced students might be expected to shoulder a greater share of this responsibility to keep their practice within the ability range of the less experienced classmates.)

Synchronized timing may seem merely an aesthetic quality to casual observers, but it can take on added significance in any context in which you engage directly with others, whether in "verbal" negotiation, push-hands practice, or outright combat/self-defense. Reflect for a moment on whether you have ever engaged in a conversation or a negotiation, perhaps one that was a bit volatile, where there was a possibility of escalating conflict. Even in a relatively benign situation, short of out-and-out combat, the timing and nuances of your remarks, not to mention your body language, can influence how events play out. Poorly crafted or ill-timed verbal communication can inflame a situation, vice de-escalating it.

Seeking the benefits of group practice.
Photo courtesy of John Loupos.

The sensitivity that you develop toward others, often unconsciously, as one consequence of group practice can help you avoid misreads and respond more effectively in resolving conflict before it gets out of control. Group practice is clearly more conducive to the acquisition of enhanced sensitivity and refined perception, for the purposes of interaction with others, than is solo practice.

From a martial perspective, the issue of timing, or synchronizing your moves to the moves of others, is especially important. Taiji as a martial art necessarily entails interaction with others, whether for prearranged push-hands practice or during actual combat or self-defense.

Nowadays, taiji is often pursued as a personal development or fitness activity with rare thought given to its fighting application. People who study taiji are often motivated to do so by reasons that are quite different from those who study harder or more external martial arts styles. Nevertheless, taiji can

155

be an effective fighting system for those who train with some regard for its martial aspects.

From a martial perspective, it is very important to know where your opponent is at all times and to be able to sense instantly if your opponent closes his distance on you. This "knowing" can stem from visually observing your opponent, or it can stem from "sensing" his or her proximity. Practicing with others, and developing an awareness of where they are at all times even in the absence of a direct visual line of contact, requires a certain peripheral awareness. This is most readily developed by practicing on a regular basis in close proximity to others. Of course, merely being able to sense an opponent's approach is useless if you lack the skills to respond accordingly, but that skill level requires preparation of a different sort.

Along these same lines, it can be instructive for any group to vary its practice speed. Learning how to keep your body properly adjusted while moving at variable speeds is essential from a martial perspective because, in a real situation, you may not be able to control the speed with which another person uses against you. Rather, you must be able to match your speed to that of your opponent. Varying the speed at which your group practices forces you to learn how to adapt to what could be a rapidly changing situation.

Seeking the benefits of individual practice.
Photo courtesy of Lin Shengxuan.

Another of the skills that group form practice teaches, even if inadvertently, is how to sense and maintain a fixed distance from those around you. Though you may have never thought of this skill as such, when you practice with others, for example in a crowded classroom, the likelihood is that you naturally become aware if someone encroaches on your space. At such times, you may automatically adjust the length or width of your step or stance, or perhaps the pace of your movements, to allow for a more manageable distance between yourself and those sharing your practice space. Taken to a more highly developed level, the same skill allows you to control and maintain a safe distance between yourself and someone who is posing a genuine threat.

Aside from the manner in which group practice prepares you for engaging with others in push-hands or combat, there is simply the shear joy of sharing your time and space with other people who are also committed to exploring the magic taiji has to offer. When you practice and train taiji, you are creating the potential to grow and evolve as a person. Such personal growth may not happen by quantum leaps, but every practice session will leave its mark in some way. Practicing *en masse* allows you and your fellow students the opportunity to learn from each other's mistakes and to share in each other's progress. Because there are few road maps outlining whatever route your personal taiji journey will take, group practice can offer solace in times of uncertainty and, in the words of Dr. Jay, "companionship along the way."

15

Sanshou:
Understanding Taijiquan as a Martial Art
by Greg Wolfson, B.A.

The author (left) playing push-hands (*tuishou*) with his teacher,
Scott M. Rodell. All photographs courtesy of Great River Taoist Center.

Introduction

The martial art taijiquan is popularly associated with the slow, graceful movements of the empty-hand form. Those with some exposure to the art might be familiar with the "push-hands" exercises (*tuishou*). In these partnered drills, each side tries to push the other off-balance using the art's eight basic techniques while maintaining physical contact. Their intent is to develop "listening energy" (*ting jin*) by feeling the strength and direction of their partner's pushes. With *tuishou*, the taiji player can practice redirecting incoming energy (in this case, pushes) without being thrust immediately into a more realistic combat environment. Few students, however, have applied these acquired skills in the "free hands" stage of training (*sanshou*), where they are tested in a full-contact, full-power environment. This is a major omission for any student wishing to learn the complete taijiquan system.

Traditionally, *sanshou* practice begins with taking individual techniques out of the empty-hand form and practicing them slowly in response to a variety of attacks. This is done repeatedly until the movement becomes natural and precise at full speed and power. From there, the student practices putting techniques together in combination. His goal here is to move freely and spontaneously from one move to the next, keeping his partner unbalanced. Eventually, the students practice full-contact play, where they must use this continuous freedom of movement to deal with whatever offense their partners bring.

This method of *sanshou* training should be differentiated from the choreographed two-person *sanshou* sets often practiced today. In these two-person forms, each player learns a set sequence of movements and then practices then in tandem with a partner, like a dance. The earliest recorded evidence of such sets within the Yang system is Chen Gong's 1932 book, *Combined Taijiquan, Broadsword, Two edged sword, Staff, and Sparring* (*Taijiquan Dao Jian Gan Sanshou Hebian*). By comparison, writings of the first three generations of Yang family masters, including transmitted instructional writings and Yang Chengfu's two books, *Complete Form and Practice of Taijiquan* (*Taijiquan Tiyong Quanshu*) and *Taijiquan Practical Methods* (*Taijiquan Shiyongfa*), contain no mention of such a form. The latter two books do contain descriptions of the other forms practiced by the Yang family, including their empty-hand, pushing-hands, saber, double-edge straight sword (*jian*), and staff forms. The existence of a two-person *sanshou* set dating back to Yang Chengfu's time would imply a glaring omission in the writings of the third-generation master.

One reason for the lack of *sanshou* training is the vast difference between the objectives of taijiquan's founders and many of today's adherents. Most students of Yang style taijiquan are unaware that the art's founder, Yang Luchan, made his living not as a taiji teacher in the contemporary sense but as a military instructor. Both he and his sons, Banhou and Jianhou, taught provincial militia and then at the military garrisons in Beijing, enjoying the patronage of Manchu princes (Wile, 1983: xi-xii). They trained soldiers at a time of great civil unrest in China; the Qing rulers had to contend with the Taiping Rebellion in the east as well as minority uprisings in the north and west. That Yang style taijiquan flourished in the military during such a period leaves little doubt as to its martial effectiveness.

Yet today, many people take up this proven art not to achieve martial excellence, as its founders intended, but to improve their health or to exercise. They want taijiquan's ability to relieve stress, revitalize their bodies, and foster a strong, calm spirit. These students wonder what participation in "violent" *sanshou* training has to do with cultivating health and calmness. They do not understand that they must practice taijiquan as a martial art in order to achieve their goals. As the taiji master Zheng Manqing said, "[Taiji] form practice that

159

ignores functional application bestows health benefits that are artificial at best" (Cheng, 1999: 6). Without an in-depth knowledge of martial technique gained from *sanshou* training, the student will not realize the vibrant health that taijiquan can produce. To understand why this is, we must explore the nature and components of the Yang family's art.

Scott M. Rodell (right) and the author developing
the "hands on" feel of taijiquan that can only
be obtained by practicing with others.

The Taijiquan System

To cultivate martial skill, taijiquan's creators developed a method of training that in many ways resembles the scientific method. Consider that in science, the scientist begins by theorizing some general principle or formula about the world. He conducts extensive research and formulates hypotheses. This is akin to the taiji player practicing the hand form. Through the form's slow, mindful movements, the player visualizes each technique's application, at the same time refining the body mechanics and internal energy (*qi*) circulation required to execute that technique.

For each technique, the practitioner imagines a training partner feeding him an idealized, slow-motion attack. The Chinese term for this partner (either real or imaginary) is *duifang*, literally "opposite direction," a term that has none of the adversarial connotations of its usual English translation, "opponent." The practitioner's responses to their *duifang* using the form postures are taiji "hypotheses." Master Zheng referred to this method when he instructed his students to "do the form as if someone is there" (Lowenthal, 1991: 109).

The next step for the scientist, once his theories are sound on paper, is to conduct laboratory experiments. He controls all aspects of the test environment, including the qualities of the test subjects and how much freedom of action they have. These procedures clarify the scientist's grasp of the principles underlying his theories.

Tuishou or "push-hands" exercises are one of the taiji player's laboratories. In these paired exercises, each partner attempts to unbalance and topple his now real *duifang* by redirecting his pushes, thereby creating openings for a counter-technique. By practicing the movements with a real person, one experiences first-hand how important precise timing and point of application are to a movement's effectiveness. The practitioner must develop a tactile sensitivity to the movements of his *duifang*, a "listening" skill that he uses to sense an incoming technique; he then responds with the appropriate counter at the appropriate time and place. Having gained this awareness of timing and distance in *tuishou*, the student can now recalibrate the actions of his imaginary *duifang* during form practice. This increases the accuracy of his responses.

The final test of the scientist is in the wild, where laboratory-tested theories are exposed to the real world's countless variations and uncertainties. As in the laboratory, the scientist analyzes this feedback and further refines his theories. For the taiji player, realizing this "real world" application is difficult (short of picking a fight). The *sanshou* or "free hands" stage of training described above closely simulates real combat with only those handicaps necessary for relative safety.

The greater distances and more precise timing of a sparring environment make *sanshou* a more difficult arena than *tuishou*. Circularizing a punch or kick from a charging *duifang* is much more challenging that redirecting pushes while in constant physical contact (as in *tuishou*). Any deficiency in one's practice, be it in body mechanics, understanding of technique, or inadequate listening skills, will greatly impair one's effectiveness. The more challenging setting forces the student to refine his understanding of distance, timing, and each of the form's martial applications.

Taijiquan and Good Health Revisited

With this broader understanding of the taijiquan system, we now have the vocabulary for linking this martial practice to the good health it promotes. When a taiji student practices the solo routine, he moves his body and circulates his internal energy (*qi*) with the express purpose of performing martial applications. The student must rigorously test his knowledge of application

161

and principle in *tuishou* and *sanshou*; otherwise, his understanding of martial technique will be shallow, improper, or even absent. Lack of focus in the solo routine will, in turn, result in a low level of internal energy development. Master T.T. Liang said that taijiquan "is a combination of civil and martial aspects," and that "neglecting either [aspect] is not a real [taijiquan]" (Liang, 1974: 54). To shun taijiquan's martial tradition (the martial aspect) is to throw away the very method of internal cultivation (the civil aspect) devised by its creators. The taijiquan practitioner obtains the desired health benefits of the art only by focusing his physical and internal development on specific martial application.

Using this training paradigm, we now turn to exploring how *sanshou* broadens the practice of taijiquan.

Push-hands is the first step in training
the spontaneous use of taijiquan's principles.

Softness and Steel

The Yang Family writings, a collection of texts expounding the principles of taijiquan, describe the advanced practitioner's body as "iron concealed in cotton" (Wile, 1983: 12). Although the player's exterior muscles are softened, they mask an inner structure of bones and sinews that is incredibly hard and powerful. This steel-like strength can be expressed at any moment to send the *duifang* flying. Many students, seeking to emulate the cotton "softness" in form practice without first improving their body mechanics, achieve only a spaghetti-like state that lacks strength and will collapse under pressure.

The Chinese term *fangsong*, which is loosely translated as "to relax" but more accurately means "to unclench the muscles," contains the proper method for cultivating this body state. First, the practitioner puts his body in order through stretching and solo routine practice, using the structure of his bones and sinews to support his body instead of external muscular tension. In particular, stretching the waist and lower back are essential to making proper knee and spine alignment possible. Without alignment, the body will collapse and lack strength when trying to execute techniques in *tuishou* or *sanshou*.

Only with this framework in place can the practitioner proceed to step two: using the mind to consciously let go of remaining muscular tension, tension accrued from a lifetime of misalignment. The student constantly monitors his body during solo routine practice and while holding postures, letting go of any unnecessary tension (for example, unshrugging the shoulders and letting the elbows hang naturally). One must be clear that the inner "iron" structure is the first requirement; only then can outer "cotton" be achieved.

This new body state increases martial skill in a variety of ways. With less obstructing muscular tension, the taiji player can more easily direct the body's movements and receive its signals. He will be able to use his waist and his internal structure to freely direct his body as one coordinated unit. This will make his steps and attacks more fluid, efficient and effortless.

As his muscles unclench further and further, the advanced practitioner will become increasingly sensitive to tactile information. If, for example, he crosses arms with a *duifang* who tries to give him a two-handed push, the taiji player's *fangsong* allows him to interpret the length and direction of this energy and begin the appropriate deflection. Less and less tension clarifies these signals until the smallest action by the other person triggers the correct response. In this way, the advanced player seems to have foreknowledge of his *duifang's* intentions. Hence the Yang family saying: "At the opponent's slightest stir, you have already anticipated it and moved beforehand" (Liang, 1974: 29).

Just as a high level of *fangsong* will increase the practitioner's effectiveness in *sanshou*, understanding the fault of stiff muscle tension will increase his ability to control his *duifang*. Consider an opposite that sticks his arm out stiffly in order to punch. This arm functions like a handle or lever connected directly to the *duifang's* spine. Executing a basic "splitting" technique (*lie*) along the line of this "lever" will disrupt the *duifang's* spine and, therefore, his entire body structure. During that moment, he becomes completely ineffective and easy to topple.

Stiffness during *sanshou* practice is not only caused by improper body mechanics; it also occurs when over-extending while "releasing energy" (*fajin*), as in a push. If one pushes to the point where the arms are fully locked, the arms tense and become handles to the spine as described above. Thus, the Yang family taijiquan writings caution that "energy should be preserved slightly [by bending the limbs somewhat] so that there is a surplus in order to avoid exhaustion" (Liang, 1974: 28). While this fault also occurs during *tuishou* practice, it is more common during *sanshou*. In the latter, the distance between players is more variable, and practitioners tend to "reach" to connect with their duifang instead of moving their body within range.

Staying Centered: Achieving Calm in Combat

Sanshou practice tests the taiji player's ability to stay calm as much as his ability to execute techniques. Cultivating this skill can pay big dividends, as Scott M. Rodell explains: "Learning not to follow thought when stung in *sanshou*, it is easier to let go in the everyday" (Rodell, 2005: 49). Conversely, if a student cannot maintain his cool and adhere to the principles during *sanshou*, he is not prepared to face a truly aggressive *duifang* or to use his practice in dealing with everyday confrontations.

How a student practices the solo routine has a dramatic effect on how well he will be prepared for tense situations. Improper solo routine practice—tensed from improper body mechanics and without martial intent—prevents students from settling and focusing either their minds, breath, or internal energy (*qi*). During *tuishou* and *sanshou*, these same practitioners tense up when pressed by their *duifangs*, anxiously resisting or dodging blows instead of calmly using their waist to direct the body and deflect the attacks.

Proper form practice cultivates the inner calm needed in the *sanshou* arena. Master T.T. Liang describes this method for moving towards calmness in his book, *T'ai Chi Ch'uan For Health and Self-Defense* (1974: 74):

Because the movement is slow, it is tranquil; because it is tranquil, the (qi) can sink deeply into the dantian and abide there; when the (qi) can sink deeply and abide in the dantian, then one can maintain oneself firmly. This is called the central equilibrium of mind and (qi). When the mind can be maintained firmly, then a calm unperturbedness can be attained ...

The taiji player begins this process by placing his mind firmly on the meridian point called the *dantian*, located three finger-widths beneath the navel. As he learns to execute the form with less tension, the player's breath and *qi* will sink naturally to the *dantian*, and he obtains this state of "central equilibrium." With the breath and *qi* concentrated, the mind will come to rest in the waist where it can consciously direct the entire body. It will then become easier and easier to maintain this cultivated mind-body state during the rigors of *sanshou*.

The author and his teacher Scott M. Rodell practicing freeform push-hands. Quick and soft, concealing internal power, techniques from taijiquan's repertoire manifest by themselves with proper training.

Victory is Achieved from the Side

Sanshou provides an opportunity to investigate techniques not easily understood through *tuishou* and form practice alone. For instance, consider the application of the movement "Step Forward, Parry Down, Punch" from Zheng Manqing's simplified form. This technique illustrates the Yang family saying "the bull's-eye is reached by attacking from the side" (Wile, 1983: 79). When the *duifang* attempts a right cross to the face, the taiji player intercepts it with his left hand and deflects it downward, redirecting his opposite's force to the right. The deflected arm becomes a lever that turns the *duifang's* body, presenting his right floating rib or "soft flank" for attack. The parry has manipulated the opposite's body and exposed his side, a position from which the he cannot quickly recover or easily counterattack. In *sanshou*, the student practices a variety of similar deflections that create openings in the *duifang's* position.

Separation and Stepping

When practicing the solo routine, the taiji player pays special attention to how he distributes or separates his weight. Each step he takes is empty, with 100% of the body's weight resting on the opposite leg. In this way, the empty or insubstantial leg is free to kick or stomp as well as step. Additionally, good separation sends the mass of the body and spine directly through the weighted leg into the ground, as if you had rammed an upright spear deep into the earth. This rooted, vertical feeling provides a proper axle around which the waist can rotate freely and direct the body.

The taiji boxer can maintain this axle as long as a majority of the body's weight is on one leg; he loses the axle when he becomes "double-weighted," meaning each leg holds 50% of the body's weight. In this situation, equal distribution of weight means the spine is equally connected in each leg. The waist now has two competing axles around which it could rotate. Just as a wheel cannot rotate around two axles, double-weighting binds the waist, restricting its freedom of motion. Consequently, the taiji player can no longer turn effectively, and all his movements will be slow and clumsy. He will not be able to adapt quickly and freely to his *duifang's* movements. While this ineffectiveness is visible in *tuishou*, it is exaggerated in *sanshou*, where the distance between combatants is greater and the timing of deflections and counters is more precise.

In addition to separation, successful stepping in *sanshou* requires a deeper understanding of another cardinal taijiquan principle, "the waist is the commander." In his *Mental Elucidation of the Thirteen Postures*, taijiquan Master Wang Zongyue states "when advancing and retreating, it is necessary to turn the body and change the steps" (Liang, 1974: 27). Master T.T. Liang explains this proper method for using the body in his commentary on this classic:

"When advancing and retreating, it is necessary to turn the body and change the steps."
– Liang, 1974: 27

When your opponent strikes the left side of your body so fast that he gives you no chance to counterattack, you must yield and turn your body slightly to the left, while stepping back with your left foot in order to regain a favorable and superior position. After you have regained a superior position, you must turn your body slightly to the right if you want to counterattack with your left hand.

Turning the body to regulate the distance between oneself and the *duifang* is impossible without first having proper separation to give the waist a definite axle to turn around. To compensate for double-weightedness and not using the waist, beginning *sanshou* students often blindly thrust their legs forward or backward when opportunity or necessity requires it. Instead of using the waist to position themselves for deflections and counters, they simply leap backwards to dodge blows or jump recklessly into perceived openings. This is an extremely imprecise and difficult way for finding a "superior position" from which they can perform techniques.

Listening Skills: Linking *Tuishou* and *Sanshou*

The taijiquan student is first introduced to the concept of "listening" (*ting jin*) during fixed-step single-hand *tuishou*. In this exercise, the two players face each other in opposing bow stances and touch forearms on the same side as their leading foot. The exercise begins when one side initiates a push anywhere above the belt and below the collar, such as pushing through their *duifang's* arm towards the right side of their body. It is then the other player's job to listen to the push through their tactile contact, deflect the incoming force and, if possible, counter.

It is important to note that *tuishou* matches aren't about swatting pushes aside and lunging at the *duifang*. The taiji player practices "sticking and following," two terms which he must understand in order to gain this tactile

167

"listening" ability. "Sticking" means that the practitioner neither loses contact with nor offers resistance against the movements of the *duifang*. In this way, one can maintain constant awareness of the *duifang's* intentions through touch.

Knowing the *duifang's* intentions alone is not enough; one must also know the proper response. "Following" means not initiating a set offense of your own but allowing your opposite's actions to determine the appropriate response. As a simple example, consider a *duifang* that strikes the taiji boxer with his left hand. One appropriate response is to execute the basic technique "split" (*lie*). Turning his waist to the right, the boxer deflects the strike to his right arm. The turning of his waist simultaneously causes the left hand to shoot out in a counterattack. Before the *duifang* attacked, there was no intent to strike from the left. The boxer simply listened to his opposite's intent and allowed the offered attack to determine his response. The *duifang* has defeated himself; the taiji boxer is simply the means to that end.

In *sanshou*, one applies the listening skills developed in *tuishou* across the greater distances of free sparring. The student must use the techniques of sticking and following, even though he is not always in physical contact with the *duifang*. The Yang family secret transcripts describe this increased ability to "interpret energy":

Only when one understands
the visual awareness of looking far,
near, left and right; the aural awareness
of rising, falling, slowness, and haste;
the kinesthetic awareness
of dodge, return, provoke and finish;
and the movement awareness of turn, exchange, advance,
and retreat, can one truly be said
to have mastered interpreting energy.
                          – Wile (Trans.), 1983: 92

Here, Rauno Gordon attempts to strike Rodell, who uses
the deflection rollback into "Brush Knee and Strike."

This full awareness of the *duifang* cannot be understood through form practice and *tuishou* alone. They simply do not provide the speed or variety of attacks that will properly season a student's understanding of how to execute taijiquan techniques. He will not learn how to stick to and follow his opponent in a manner not bounded by tactile contact.

In *tuishou*, the student must stick to his *duifang* continuously, always ready to respond appropriately to an attack or retreat. In *sanshou*, the situation is no different. Usually, the beginner will stick and adapt until he takes the offensive, at which point the greater distances of *sanshou* will force him to overreach and lock his arms (as described in the section on *fangsong*). Tensing up in this fashion makes it difficult for the student to remain calm and aware of his *duifang*, and he cannot respond appropriately if his opposite deflects and counters. The Yang family writings were aware of this possibility, and cautioned that "the energy may be broken off [i.e. discharged], but the mind-intent remains" (Liang, 1974: 30). Even when the taiji player discharges into his *duifang*, he must remain mentally connected to him, aware of his position and intent and ready to continue adapting.

Rodell intercepts the attack with this left elbow and swings
his left forearm downward, creating an opening on the neck for his right hand.
A circular movement right wardoff off-balances the attacker into an effortless throw.

Sticking continuously also allows the taiji player to maintain the initiative when on the offensive. The reality is that in *sanshou*, the sparring is almost never ended with only one strike; a combination of counters that act as one is necessary to subdue the *duifang*. If the *sanshou* player is always aware of his *duifang's* position and intent, he can keep constant pressure on his opposite and maintain the upper hand. A focused series of attacks based on continuously sticking to and following the *duifang* will be increasingly difficult to neutralize. The taiji player's listening skills allow him to be a step ahead of his partner's deflections, forcing the latter to deal with a new attack before he has even recovered from the previous one. Yang Luchan, the founder of Yang style taijiquan, called this "movement like a mighty river" (Wile, 1983: 109), bowling over the hapless *duifang*. With such skill, victory is a matter of discerning opportunity.

1

2

3

Chinese	Terms
dantian	丹田
duifang	對方
fajin	發勁
fangsong	鬆
lie	挒
qi	氣
sanshou	散手
taijiquan	太極拳
ting jin	聽勁
tuishou	推手

Acknowledgment

Special thanks to Great River Taoist Center and teacher Scott M. Rodell for all the training, editorial input, and inspiration. All push-hands photographs courtesy of Tim Fenoglio.

171

Bibliography

Chen, Gong (1943). *Taijiquan dao jian gan sanshou hebian* (Combined taijiquan, broadsword, two edged sword, staff, and sparring). n.p.

Cheng, Man-ching (1999). *Master Cheng's new method of t'ai chi self-cultivation.* Trans. Mark Hennessy. Berkeley, CA: North Atlantic Books.

Liang, T. (1974). *T'ai chi ch'uan for health and self-defense.* New York: Vintage Books.

Lowenthal, W. (1991). *There are no secrets: Professor Cheng Man-Ch'ing and his tai chi chuan.* Berkeley, CA: North Atlantic Books.

Rodell, S. (2005). *Taiji notebook for martial artists.* Annandale, VA: Seven Stars Books and Video.

Wile, D. (Trans.). (1983). *T'ai-chi touchstones: Yang family secret transmissions.* Brooklyn, NY: Sweet Ch'i Press.

Yang, Chengfu (1931). *Taijiquan shiyongfa* (Taijiquan practical methods). n.p. Reprinted as Taijiquan Yongfa Tujie. Taipei: Wuzhou Chu-banshi, 1996.

Yang, Chengfu (1934). *Taijiquan tiyong quanshu* (Complete form and practice of taijiquan). Hong Kong, n.p. Reprinted, Taipei: Wu Xue guan (Lion Books), 2001.

16

Benefits of Non-Competitive Push-Hands Practice
by Herman P. Kauz

Photograph courtesy of Akiko O. Dykhuizen.

Introduction

In recent years we have learned about the health benefits of taijiquan (usually shortened to taiji). *Taiji* means to most of us a slow motion set of connected movements resembling boxing, performed solo. It is widely practiced in China, especially by older people. Chinese city parks are filled early each morning with people doing various forms of exercise, a strong contingent of taiji practitioners among them. This practice strengthens legs, improves balance, calms the mind and spirit, and generally improves mental and physical health.

Related to this solo form exercise is a practice called push-hands. Here two persons face one another and attempt to break one another's balance using only a minimum of strength. It is generally done slowly from a fixed foot position. That is, if you are losing your balance, stepping in any direction to regain it is incorrect. The couple then breaks off and returns to a few moves of a simple form which precedes a freer style of attack and counterattack.

The reason we generally practice with a fixed foot position is that our response in both attack and defense comes primarily from a change in our body position and not through a foot movement. We must react to an attack by shifting our center and by yielding to the slightest pressure. The "center" is that point on the body where our opponent can control us. This point is constantly shifting as the opponent attempts to break our balance and as we try to evade.

As an attack is mounted, the defender not only neutralizes it but attempts simultaneously to counterattack. The attacker is somewhat vulnerable to a counter as he gets to that point in his forward movement where his weight is equally distributed between his feet. This is termed "double weighting" and results in a temporarily weakened position. If the defender counterattacks at this point, the attacker must neutralize it and continue the attack. We say that attacking is yang and defending is yin. But as we see in the taiji circle, yang has a small circle of yin in it, and yin a small circle of yang. Thus, while the defender mainly yields (*yin*) he also at the right moment counters (*yang*). The attacker is mostly yang, but he yields (*yin*) to the defender's countermove.

These attacks and counters often occur in split seconds. Though we attempt to practice slowly, our opponent may suddenly speed up, and we must keep pace. Another complication lies in our attempt to use only a minimum of strength to attack or to counter. Often we use more than a few ounces of pressure in whatever we do, allowing a more skillful opponent to use this over-doing against us. We try then to be rooted in our feet and to be relaxed and flexible from the ankles up. We might think of the body as a piece of hanging cloth which absorbs and neutralizes an incoming force without harm. The attacker might then overextend and lose balance, expecting a solid surface and meeting no resistance.

Photographs by Donna Bernardini.

The relaxed alertness and calmness gained from solo form practice is clearly going to be more difficult to maintain when your partner is trying to upset your balance. If we sense aggressiveness from our partner or an unwillingness to yield, we may become angry. All of the difficulties we may have in dealing with others in daily life will gradually make an appearance. If we are open to it, we can learn a great deal about ourselves in push-hands.

Most of us, as nothing we do works to our satisfaction, will experience some degree of frustration. We will try to follow our teacher's suggestion to avoid both resisting a push and pushing into hardness. Our teacher will show many times that resisting a push to maintain our balance will cause the opponent to instantly attack from a different direction and the game will be over. Also, attacking a point that seems unyielding with more strength gives the opponent a chance to suddenly yield, causing our overextension and loss of balance.

When a problem comes up in our daily life, we try to think of a solution. Logical, linear thought might be of some use in trying to figure out what is going on in push-hands. But in the moment the action occurs any advance planning or strategy will probably fail because you can't predict the opponent's response. Moreover, trying to think in push-hands will cause one's body to tense while figuring things out. More importantly, as beginners, we are limited in awareness and are often too hard, too tense, or our timing is faulty. So even if we do our best to follow our teacher's directions, we are incapable of doing what is required. To begin to get a sense of what is going on, our awareness and sensitivity must grow and sharpen. This is a never ending process. Continuing to make progress in this direction requires almost daily push-hands practice. But, if we practice incorrectly, by using strength, for example, our progress will be slow or nonexistent. What is ultimately required is an internalization by our physical and mental systems of an instant thought-free response to the slightest stimulus. Moreover, to be successful, our response must consist of an optimum mix of softness, sensitivity, and timing, to name just a few qualities.

The process resembles that experienced by the Zen archery student, who must practice endlessly to loose a shot which he does not let go consciously. Instead, in a particular moment the archer, the bow, the arrow, and the target become one. To cite another example, the solution to a Zen koan cannot be rationally arrived at, but must come in some other way. In both archery and Zen, the student does all he can to get a hoped for result. This means he will use his mental and physical ability to do what seems to be required, only to have his efforts rejected or deemed unsuccessful. This sad state of affairs may last a few years, but his efforts, or non-efforts, may one day bear fruit, only to be followed by a further period of failure.

Focusing again on push-hands, common student errors are failing to find the opponent's center, using too much strength, resisting an attack and trying to think their way through the pushing process. If our opponent is more skillful than we, every pushing encounter will result in failure. This outcome can be quite frustrating, unless the student comes to the training with no expectations or preconceived ideas and is willing to be open to what unfolds as he attempts to follow taiji principles. There is really no final goal—it is an endless refining process.

It is really only an illusion that the sought for result in push-hands is to push the opponent or to avoid a push. Instead, we should be trying to react in a thought-free way to what our system senses in the moment. This pattern stops the stream of thought having to do with past or future and puts us, if even for a little while, fully in the present. Halting our incessant mind chatter is a marvelous method for opening us to a sense of the spirit (or whatever one wants to call it) that permeates or suffuses us and everything around us. This aspect of push-hands may seem a bit too extreme or esoteric for some, but it is there for those who are ready for it. The benefits for our lives with this emphasis far outweigh those which accrue from limiting ourselves to just the physical.

Push-hands training then can be regarded as learning to become more responsive and more sensitive. To help us in this direction, all our attacking and defending moves should be limited to a mere few ounces of pressure. If we employ even a little too much force, a skillful opponent will use our overdoing against us. Also, all we need do is to unbalance our opponent. The instant this occurs, were it a self-defense situation, we could deliver a further attack to a vulnerable point. Pushing someone 10 or 20 feet away is regarded, from a practical standpoint, as losing your opponent. Unless he is at the edge of a cliff, he has a chance to regroup or to avail himself of a weapon and then return to the fray.

If our reason for doing push-hands is to develop improved fighting ability, we could well retard our development of the more important responsiveness and sensitivity we seek. It is true that push-hands practice can lay a superb foundation for fighting arts, but too great an emphasis on fighting techniques as we do push-hands will make us harder. I taught a kind of self-defense to taiji students for over 20 years, in an attempt to familiarize them with attacks from punches, strikes, and kicks. I don't think this training helped much to improve students' abilities in push-hands, though it gave them some measure of self-defense ability.

At any rate, we are far better served, in terms of positive benefits, by developing our sensitivity. Even for martially oriented individuals, gaining additional awareness and acting in a timely way to defuse a situation is far superior to having to physically engage an opponent.

As our push-hands develops over the years, we may be fortunate enough to encounter a highly developed practitioner who offers no resistance and whose center is unavailable. While we are searching for some slight degree of solidity, we find we have overextended and somehow have lost our balance. If we use more strength and speed, the result is worse. Everyone who does push-hands seems to approve of softness and yielding and even to believe that is how they are pushing. An actual experience with someone who is really skilled may open our eyes to the vast possibilities for development in the physical aspects of push-hands. Of course, we will want to know how we can reach this higher level. The answer is to give up strength, and to "invest in loss," as Zheng Manqing (1902-1975) put it. By this he meant avoid all resistance and try to learn from each push.

We are also faced with another problem. Language is inadequate to express what goes on in push-hands. This statement sounds like nonsense, but try as we might we really can't put into words what is happening in a particular moment. We can talk about the moment before it occurs and after it has occurred, but in the instant something happens our trained physical and mental system responds, either successfully or not. Many factors come together in a particular moment and thinking about what is happening will inhibit movement. We might well become frozen and fail to move at the right time. Essentially, we will have lost the flow.

A few hurdles, some rather high, stand in the way of our practicing to rise to a higher level. Among them are such handicaps as a strong body, skill in other martial arts, and a competitive turn of mind. One's system will respond to an emergency by doing what it has been trained to do. Changing a previous conditioning is the work of many years. Reverting to what our systems have previously learned will keep those connections alive and functioning. New connections must form in the brain and in our body if our response is going to change. These slowly form as we practice correctly over the years. If we can't give up what we have, we will fail to move in the direction we believe we want to go, no matter how long and hard we practice.

Our competitive culture has spawned push-hands contests. The Chinese also engage in such competition. Training to win such a contest will probably produce a different attitude toward push-hands than if "winning" in an encounter is of no consequence. We will tend to use strength, become ruthless, and generally ignore or give only lip service to the push-hands advice found in the taiji classics.

Push-hands styles range from a kind of Japanese sumo wrestling to the very sensitive. The classics state that if even a fly lights on your shoulder, your body should be set in motion. It takes many years of practice to develop the ability to perform in this lighter and more responsive way. But our impatience for results and craving for success will lead to our resisting pushes and to using too much strength. Possibilities for mental and spiritual growth are present in all martial arts. But when these arts are practiced as sport, the emphasis is on winning. Taijiquan practice is also vulnerable to this interpretation. There is no question in my mind that this approach, unfortunately, precludes the attainment of the kind of development we say we are seeking.

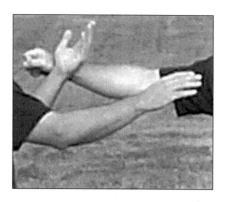

Photographs by Donna Bernardini.

My teacher, Zheng Manqing, among others, spoke of push-hands as a precious gem. He would teach everyone the taiji solo form because it would improve their health. But he refused to teach everyone push-hands. Those of us who practice correctly over the decades would probably also come to the conclusion that we have been given something of great value.

17

Form and Function: Why Push-Hands Is Essential to the Practice of Taijiquan
by Hal Mosher, B.A.

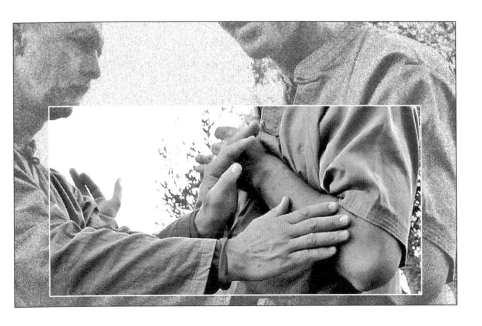

Allen Pittman (left) and Hal Mosher pushing-hands.

Introduction

Push-hands practice is often overlooked or misunderstood by taiji practitioners. Many allow the exercise to devolve into a mere shoving contest, missing the nuance and multilayered complexity of this vehicle for researching yielding, the heart of taijiquan. The great importance of push-hands lies in the use of yielding against an attack without using force, following the movements of one's opponent with acute sensitivity, and remaining firmly rooted and balanced in the process. When push-hands is practiced correctly with a partner, one may quickly discover problem areas, such as a lack of responsive shifting, the use of force, holding unnecessary tension in the body, the use of too much upper-body strength ("double heaviness" in taiji), and the lack of root or strength in the legs ("double lightness").

Immediate and valuable feedback is experienced when one is pushed off balance as a result of committing one or more of these errors. These problem areas may also be present in one's solo taiji form, and they can become easily ingrained through repetition if not corrected. Thus, push-hands helps to test the degree of embodiment of the taiji principles in one's solo form. It highlights the faults in one's postures. The process of identifying and correcting these faults will greatly improve the quality of one's form and application.

One of the main focuses of taijiquan training is to clearly differentiate substantial (representing an aspect of *yang*) and insubstantial (representing an aspect of *yin*). The goal is to embody the yin and yang symbol by keeping substantial and insubstantial elements in balance throughout all movements. While practicing push-hands, a dynamic exchange of yin and yang is created between the two partners. If one person uses too much force (*yang*), then the other must yield to that force (*yin*) and bring the mutual dynamic back into balance. As this practice becomes more refined, one will develop the ability to feel one's partner become imbalanced even before he commits to an attack. At this level, one may learn to yield in a more timely and complete fashion. If one person is imbalanced, then the partner has to bring yin and yang back into balance, which often results in the over extended partner being "pushed out" or thrown off balance in an apparently effortless way.

Push-hands helps one develop very specific martial skills—primarily the ability to quickly recognize the weight distribution of one's opponent. It uses the postures of the taiji form to create weakness in an opponent through imbalance, and allows for the conversion of the opponent's force into a counterattack. This practice is especially effective against a throw. The weight shift required for the throw to be executed will become obvious to the push-hands practitioner, even before it fully occurs, thereby allowing one to respond swiftly with a countermeasure, all while remaining firmly rooted. The opponent will give away the game plan without even knowing it.

The Basic Principles of Push-Hands

When beginning push-hands practice, both partners face one another with only a few inches of separation and both palms touching the creases of the other partner's elbows. The legs are bent and shoulder width apart; one foot is positioned ahead of the other. Both partners begin shifting forward and back until one partner goes off balance.

This close contact interaction tests one's ability to stay centered when an opponent is in very close proximity. This spatial disadvantage can be turned into an advantage through the over extension and ultimate "pushing out" of one's opponent while remaining balanced and centered. Response training of this kind is not common in most other systems of martial arts, where the emphasis is placed on strength to overcome an opponent. Push-hands uses relaxation and waist flexibility to respond to an attack, not force. This flexibility and slow turning of the waist at close range gives one the ability to easily absorb and redirect the weight and movement of one's opponent instead of struggling to counter it with arm strength.

The movements of solo practice in taijiquan must be fine, continuous, slow, and even. When applying this to push-hands, the goal is to feel this kind of continuous movement throughout the body while pushing with a partner. The response to a push should be as above: slow, continuous, soft, and even. If a person's push-hands partner moves hard and fast, one will be able to meet this speed with agility and softness to bring that mutual dynamic of yin and yang back into balance.

The absorption of a partner's weight is accomplished by taking that energy and transferring it into one's hands, letting it then travel through the body until it reaches the "full" weighted foot (containing all of, or the majority of, one's weight). Once it reaches the "full" foot, it is transferred again through the body and returned to the partner. This is much like pushing down on the coil of a spring—the energy given is returned with the same force. This is how yielding and pushing work together as a single technique. There should be softness in the upper body while the lower body is strong and heavy. This upper-body softness is what allows yielding, while the strong lower body stays rooted, resulting in the unbalancing of one's partner.

Yielding, Not Forcing

After a while, the push-hands practitioner will start to notice that a minimal amount of physical strength is needed to push a partner. As advised in the taiji classics, each partner should put forth only four ounces of force. Four ounces is, of course, impossible to actually measure when pushing, but is used more as a reminder of how little force is necessary. As mentioned above, the idea in push-hands is to avoid using the strength of the arms to push. For this to happen, all previous knowledge about pushing has to be transformed into movement that is generated by the shifting of one's weight and the turning of one's waist. The taijiquan classics state, "If there is a problem in responding to an attack, look for the source of the problem and the antidote in the waist and legs." When yielding is done properly, the result will be the redirection of the partner's energy.

Every push has a source, and the push-hands practitioner is constantly attuned to this. If the opponent pushes by using only one side of the body, then the push originates on the opposite side. The majority of the time, the upper body of one's partner is moving well ahead of the lower body, so one only needs to push the lower body to cause an imbalance. For example, when the partner's left shoulder leads during the push, one can yield by turning one's waist to the right and pushing on the partner's right hip to cause the upset (the partner's energy continues to flow in a circular motion and is only being helped along that path.) A person should only move in response to one's partner, no more and no less. Practicing push-hands this way will greatly increase one's ability to sense and follow the movements of a pushing partner.

Absorbing the Push

When one's partner pushes, the push must be followed and absorbed into the sacrum in order to remain centered. One can think of the energy going into the sacrum like catching a ball. Once the weight enters the sacrum, it is pulled down and tucked slightly forward in a "rolling under" type of movement. The energy then goes down one's "full" leg and comes out through the opposite hand. As in the aforementioned coiled spring description, when moving only in proportion to the partner's movement, one can take the energy that is coming forward in the push, absorb it, and then redirect the energy safely away. As long as a yield—not force—is used to deflect an attack, then the cycle of yin and yang in the push and yield process will be successfully completed.

Double Heaviness and Double Lightness

These are both faults that occur in push-hands practice. Double heaviness (too much tension in both the upper and lower body) makes the form too hard or limp. Double lightness (not being firmly rooted in the legs and a collapsed upper body) creates floating and makes the form dysfunctional while pushing. The right combination of lightness (empty, without tension) and heaviness (sinking) in one's practice is what creates the ability to yield and respond with the proper amount of force. The lower body should be thought of as "heavy" while, in contrast, the upper body is "light." This is done by bending one's knees deeply and remaining upright and centered. The most common error in push-hands practice is heaviness in the upper body and lightness in the lower body. Each time the weight shifts onto one leg, there is heaviness going down the outside of the leg while lightness comes up the inside of the leg. This sinking is very active and quite subtle at the same time and requires relaxation while practicing, especially during push-hands. If one's upper body remains soft and light, then the push coming from the partner is easily absorbed as the waist turns and the legs remain firmly rooted. Essentially, the partner has nothing to actually "push"—no hardness to stop the momentum of the energy that will continue to move forward, resulting in overextension and imbalance. By contrast, if one's upper body is tense and the lower body is heavy, one is then "double heavy" and can be easily toppled by an effective push.

Every part of the body has its "full" and "empty" aspect, depending on the posture, in solo taiji practice and in push-hands. While practicing with a partner, if both hands are equally hard, they are double weighted. To avoid this, one hand must be light (empty, or relaxed) and the other heavy (full, or dynamic). The hand that is heavy, or full, is the opposite one of the leg that is full (for example, if the right leg is full, then the left hand is full). This sensitivity to yin and yang in one's partner will become honed into different ways of dealing with the angle of an attack. If one can yield by relaxing the side of the body that is being pushed, then the push will drop into the waist. As the waist turns, the push will be transferred to one's opposite side. This will help in the distinguishing of full and empty in the left and right sides of the body, and will become clear in the upper and lower body over time through practice.

The Four Directions of Yielding

There are four ways to deal with an attack in push-hands, or four directions in which to yield. The first way is by using "the square." This is when a partner pushes on the side of a person's body (left or right), one returns the push using one's opposite side. The points of the square are the shoulders and hips. This is the most basic way of yielding by turning off the centerline, and is used in most other martial arts systems. The second way is using "the circle," also called "wardoff." The arms are used as a shield that turns horizontally to protect the centerline. When the attack comes in, one would rotate on the circle of the attack. The circle will always defeat the square. The third way is "the sphere," which uses the circle in three dimensions. When an opponent attacks on the surface of the sphere, then the attack is returned. This way is unique to taiji and is equated with the down/up turn and left/right turn together. The sphere can defeat both the circle and the square. The fourth is "the point." The point combines all three techniques in one indistinct posture. The yielding and attacking happen simultaneously and effortlessly. The point can overcome any of the first three attacks.

Guide to Practicing Push-hands

There are some general guidelines that a push-hands practitioner should follow during practice:

- The arms should never be disconnected from the waist and root. Instead, allow the whole body to be used to absorb an attack. The arms and hips move together with one turn.
- A circular approach should be used to aid in yielding and pushing. If one's partner pushes straight ahead, then one can turn the waist and make the attack circular.
- One should not make the mistake of overextending, creating holes, gaps, or discontinuity. A hole is created when one is pulling on a partner. Gaps are formed when one's hands are too far apart. And, discontinuity happens when not all body parts are connected to the turn or weight shift.
- One should not try to win, but just listen and feel. Push-hands is not sumo wrestling. Partners must agree not to use too much force and instead learn to yield. If one's partner uses excessive force, the attack should be side-stepped and not confronted. Excessive force always results in the bigger person being victorious, and no skills are acquired that way. The skill one is trying to attain is yielding, not punching or kicking. This is why the concept of using four ounces is so important when practicing push-hands.

PUSH AND ROLLBACK TRAINING EXERCISES

Sensitivity training

All two-person taiji practices highlight sensitivity to movement and the shifting of weight. The following exercises are to be done very slowly in the beginning, with an emphasis on softness in order to help develop awareness of the whole body.

1) Playing the Piano One Finger at a Time

This is the simplest way to develop "listening skills."

a) A puts one hand on B's chest at sternum level. B stands upright with all weight on one leg. A gently pushes one finger into his chest while B turns away from that finger. B should only move in response to A's push and keep contact with A's finger, even as it retreats (this technique is called "following" or "sticking").

b-c-d) A then chooses the next finger and repeats the process. A repeats the same exercise with the ring and then the pinky fingers. It is important for person A to go slowly and to choose only one finger at a time until B becomes used to responding.

B is receiving the real practice of listening while at the same time strengthening his leg, so both partners should play the roles of A and B. This exercise will teach the different angles that one must be aware of when yielding to a push.

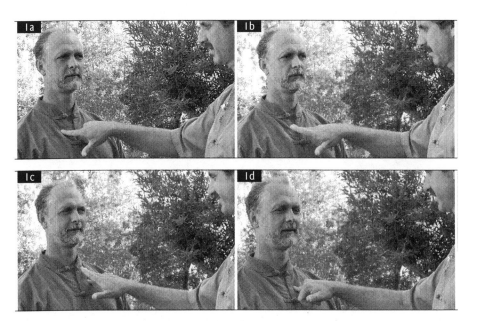

2) Pushing Four Corners

This exercise is similar to the previous exercise, but instead involves pushing on the four corners with one hand (two shoulders and two hips). In this case, 1) person A pushes on B's right shoulder, then 2) left shoulder, 3) right hip, and then 4) left hip.

During all of this, B has all weight on one leg with both hands relaxed at his sides. B yields to person A by turning with the push and not resisting it. As above, after yielding to the push, B will "follow" person A's hand and keep contact with it as it retreats. This same process is repeated with the other three corners. Switch roles with person A. This practice is used to learn how to yield and follow.

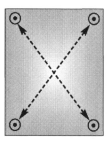

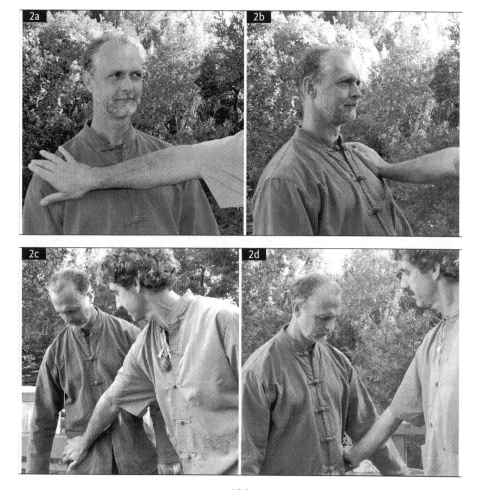

Single-Hand Push, Weighted on One Leg

This is a modified version of a one-handed push-hands practice as taught by Zheng Manqing. In this practice, both A and B have full weight on one leg throughout the practice.

1) Both A and B stand with their right legs at front. A pushes with his right palm toward B's right shoulder.
2) B starts turning to the right.
3) As B's hand comes close to A's shoulder, A turns further to the right.
4-5-6) The roles are then reversed, starting with B pushing and A turning his waist in order to yield to the incoming force.
7) The cycle is continued with A pushing and B neutralizing.
8-9) Now B is pushing and A is neutralizing.

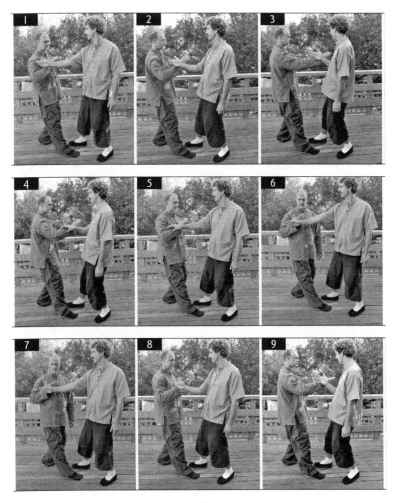

Partners should both switch legs and hands to practice both sides. This exercise is done to emphasize moving the arm with the waist and eventually the whole body as a unit. It also helps the two participants learn to be connected, in this case at the wrists. Here, movement is generated by the waist via rotation of the thighs. As one's thighs rotate, the arms must move in direct proportion to them. In order to practice central equilibrium, the sacrum must be vertical and lined up with one's feet.

One Person Pushing

This training exercise only uses the two-hand push technique, where one person pushes while the other receives the push.

1) B has all the weight on one leg while A stands in front of B with the same foot forward in a 70–30% stance. If there is a wall nearby, B should get pushed with his back to the wall so he can gently fall against it. (Having a surface close by helps one relax and let go of the fear of falling.) A then pushes on B's left arm resting on his body.

2) A pushes slowly and gently until B's front foot lifts off the ground. A then backs off his push to let B's foot down. This is done to show that even in push there is an element of yielding. Repeat three times to person B.

3) The third time, A pushes B gently against the wall as B's body comes back into A's hands. B is not completely passive, however; he tries to hide his center while being pushed, and to stick to person A. More important, B tries to relax his natural tendency to tense up when being pushed. A is trying to make the gap between B's rising up and his foot dropping imperceptible. B should not feel A go back at all and should just feel him relax.

4) If this sequence is done correctly, B will bounce like a ball before hitting the wall. This happens because lifting up B's foot and then letting him come back uproots him.

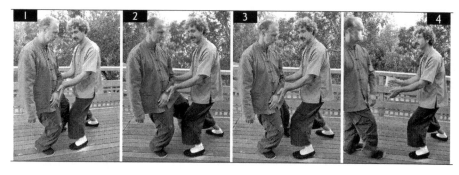

After three pushes on each side, the roles are switched.

In the beginning, A might feel resistance in B; he may resist putting all of his weight on one leg. Most people resist being pushed. The antidote is to shift back and forth until both partners relax into the momentum and movement. The goal of this practice is to yield completely when being pushed. A should be trying to push at different angles and notice the quality of push each time. The less force used to push, the better the quality of the push.

One Person Rollback

1) A and B are facing each other in a 70–30% stance, with B pushing and A doing rollback.

2) B fully commits to his push and over-extends into A's rollback. A then sits on his back leg, taking all of B's weight into it.

3) When the weight is fully received, A does rollback by turning his waist.

4) This should push person *B* off diagonally if done correctly. This technique reinforces the need to yield completely before rollback can be done effectively.

5) Once *A* has all of his weight on his back leg, he needs to find more "space" in his foot for partner *B*'s weight—so, essentially, going as far into the yield as possible without falling back, and then yielding just a little more. *A* does this by continuing to move the rear thigh forward, creating the circle needed to move the opposite arm in rollback. This practice combines using central equilibrium to remain upright, and the absorption of the push.

Push and Rollback Together

   This last exercise combines push and rollback together as one unit of movement with both partners equally engaged in each activity. One person will push or rollback, depending on the situation.

1-2) If person A overextends, then B does rollback.

3-4) Person A will push and B will respond with rollback; then person B will respond with a push while person A does rollback. The movements should be light, with both partners following one another while shifting back and forth together, like a pendulum. This exercise is spontaneous and without set limits, so partners must not use force. It is recommended that the first four exercises be mastered before moving on to this practice. When done with softness, this practice becomes an easy way to develop listening skills and an ability to follow one's opponent completely to anticipate his movements. This is the pinnacle of push-hands practice.

Conclusion

As a taijiquan practitioner, one can use the skills of acute sensitivity to an opponent's movements along with the ability to read and follow those movements effectively as the basis for understanding and redirecting an attack. A major goal is to overextend an opponent by yielding to his or her own momentum. Once this is accomplished, then any attack (a pull, strike, or throw) can be easily applied while one's opponent is off-balance. Shifting and turning the waist allow more response time and directional flexibility when yielding, and sinking will allow one to remain balanced and centered. This is where the proper embodiment of the taiji form becomes essential to push-hands; thus the solo form and the partner drills become important symbiotic practices.

Acknowledgment

This chapter is dedicated to my push-hands teacher, Mr. Liu Xiheng (a senior student of Zhang Manqing). Thanks goes to Allen Pittman for his good-natured participation in the photographs for the technical section, and a very heartfelt thank you to Laura Ballard—her hard work, dedication, and encouragement are what made this chapter possible.

18

Wardoff, Diagonal Flying from Zheng-Style Taijiquan

by Russ Mason, M.A.

Practical Applications of Taiji's Ward-Off and Diagonal Flying Postures

Ward-off is one of the fundamental postures of Yang-style taijiquan. The Chinese character for ward-off is *peng*, an obscure pictogram containing elements representing "hand" and "twin moons" reflecting each other as "friends." Another theory posits that the origin of *peng* may be a primitive character for the tail of the legendary phoenix, a bird symbolic of natural harmony and yin-yang balance. Both images present a good metaphor for the principles of sticking and following, which are essential to the application of taiji boxing. As a signature technique of the art, ward-off employs *peng jin*, an outwardly expanding energy that is further developed in the diagonal flying posture. Applications of the ward-off left and diagonal flying postures will be illustrated here.

Zheng Manqing was a disciple of Yang Chengfu and the creator of the thirty-seven-posture Yang short form, which he taught to my instructors who, in turn, passed the art to me. Zheng taught that the ultimate principle of taijiquan resides in the application of neutralization and the substance of central equilibrium (*zhong ding*). Attacking energy is received and, through yielding and neutralizing, redirected around one's constant central axis. Therefore, the principles of neutralization, sticking, and following permeate every application of taijiquan. Accordingly, the ward-off posture is primarily soft, receptive, and perceptive (like a cricket's antenna); however, ward-off energy (an expanding energy that rises upward and outward) can be used to issue energy as well as to sense it.

While learning the solo form as a beginning taijiquan student, my first encounter with ward-off left me puzzled. Since I had heard that taijiquan eschews blocking, the use of this posture seemed mysterious until I experienced its application at the hands of Zheng Manqing's senior student, Benjamin Pang Jeng Lo. At a workshop hosted by Robert W. Smith in the 1970s, I had a chance to cross arms with Mr. Lo. As soon as he touched me, to my astonishment, I felt completely vulnerable, as if through that contact he could perceive my intentions. His eyes dancing with amusement, Mr. Lo used his soft wardoff arm to totally control me, literally wiping the floor with my sprawling body. Two decades later, my understanding of the function deepened as Liu Xiheng, head of Zheng's Taipei school, used his profoundly relaxed wardoff arm and an almost imperceptible whole-body movement to effortlessly receive my attack and send me flying several meters away.

In applying wardoff, one must remain soft, alert, and sensitive. The body is relaxed, rooted, and balanced, always maintaining central equilibrium. First, one must receive and yield to the opponent's attack, perceiving its force and direction and following the attacker's intention. After the attack has been neutralized and controlled, the attacker's body will be disordered and unbalanced, leaving an opportunity for counterattack. One must be careful not to resist force with force. By joining with rather than blocking the attacking limb, the energy of the attack can be stored and returned.

The diagonal flying posture appears in only a right-handed version in Professor Zheng's system. It consists of a more complex series of transitional movements culminating in a flamboyant extended attack that extrapolates the ideas introduced by ward-off. I vividly remember the moment of stunned terror I felt when Robert W. Smith applied this technique with a lightning fast thrust to my throat, gripping my trachea expertly and inextricably between his thumb and index finger. His firm but gentle grasp did not injure me, but left no doubt in my mind of the potential lethality of the technique.

The diagonal flying posture includes a deep, 135-degree step and turn, suggesting a wide range of movement, and the hands move through splitting, tearing, and piercing actions. Finally, the articulation of the right arm and the waist suggests a "folding" technique in which the downward energy of an arm grab above the elbow is converted circularly to a thrusting attack by folding the elbow down and extending the hand forward.

The final piercing extension of the upturned palm in diagonal flying can be used to attack the throat by spearing, grasping, or striking. The "V" created by the right thumb and index finger of the upturned right hand can grasp the cricoid cartilage surrounding the opponent's larynx and thyroid, or slightly below that, where the trachea meets the larynx. The first joint of the index finger can apply pressure to the common carotid artery as the thumb presses into the windpipe or internal jugular vein. Alternatively, the posture may be used to lock the opponent's right arm or, with an outward rotation of the palm, forearm, and waist, the technique can be modified to create an unbalancing deflection or a throw using the knife edge of the downturned hand against the side of the neck.

Like wardoff, diagonal flying can be an effective counter to a right or left punch, or a front kick. The essence of the application is in yielding and following, so the exact articulation of the counterattack depends on the situation and the opponent's responses.

Technique 1: Wardoff

1a) Russ Mason neutralizes Erik Flannigan's left punch, controlling the arm with wardoff's transitional "hold the ball" stance. 1b) After blending with and sticking to the attack, Mason shifts and follows Flannigan's retreat, stepping in and controlling his balance with wardoff. 1c) Mason sits deeply into wardoff to uproot and discharge Flannigan.

1d) Alternatively, Mason neutralizes Flannigan's right punch. 1e) Mason unbalances Flannigan and shifts weight to the right foot while pivoting left, throwing him.

Technique 2: Diagonal Flying

2a) Mason neutralizes Flannigan's right front kick, capturing the leg. 2b) He uses diagonal flying to attack Flannigan's throat, immobilizing his right leg and controlling his balance. 2c) Mason uses a throat attack to unbalance and throw Flannigan. 2d) Alternatively, Mason uses diagonal flying against his right punch to lock Flannigan's arm and break his root. 2e) Mason uses a knife-edge hand and whole-body power against Flannigan's neck to unbalance and throw him.

Thanks to colleague Erik Flannigan (3rd dan TKD) for assistance with the demonstrations and to Laurie Fuhrmann for the photography.

index

82241873R00113

Made in the USA
Columbia, SC
16 December 2017